COMPLEMENTS OF

SOUVENIR GUIDE TO DALLAS TEXAS

D. M. ANDERSON DIRECTORY CO.

J. M. COLVILLE, FRANKLIN PRINTING HOUSE, DALLAS.

Marula

An imprint of Arcadia Publishing

Souvenir Guide to Dallas, Texas
A Sketch of Dallas and Dallas County, Their Resources, Business Enterprises, Manufacturing and Agricultural Advantages. With a Directory of the Leading Business Firms and Professional Men.

D.M. Anderson Directory Company

A Marula Historical Reprint
Originally published in 1894

Published by Arcadia Publishing
Charleston SC

ISBN 978-0-7385-9485-9

Printed in the United States of America

For all general information contact Arcadia Publishing at:
Telephone 843-853-2070
Fax 843-853-0044
E-mail sales@arcadiapublishing.com
For customer service and orders:
Toll-Free 1-888-313-2665

Visit us on the Internet at www.arcadiapublishing.com

SOUVENIR GUIDE

OF

DALLAS,

A Sketch of Dallas and Dallas County, their resources, business enterprises, manufacturing and agricultural advantages.

—WITH—

A Directory of the leading Business Firms and Professional Men.

Compiled and Published by

THE D. M. ANDERSON DIRECTORY COMPANY,

No. 282 Main Street.

DALLAS, - - TEXAS.

DALLAS, TEXAS:
J. M. COLVILLE'S FRANKLIN PRINT.
1894.

PADGITT BROS.

MANUFACTURERS AND JOBBERS OF

SADDLERY

In All Its Branches.

SADDLERY HARDWARE, LEATHER, TREES, ETC.

Carry a Large and Assorted Stock of

BUGGIES,

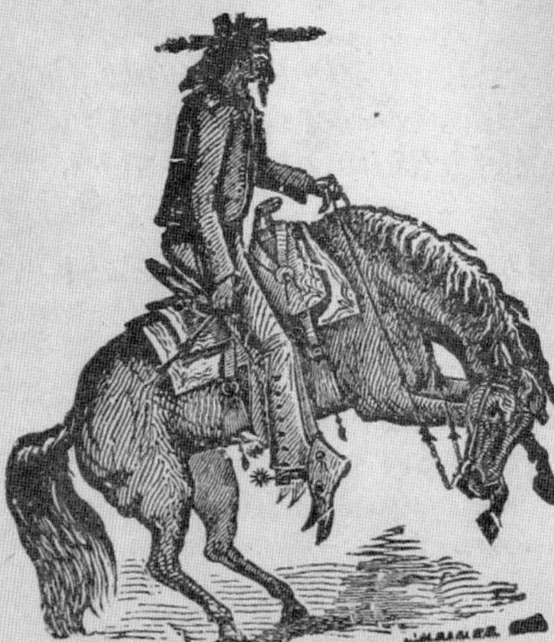

Carts,

ROAD

AND

Machine

Wagons,

Buggy Tops,

Umbrellas,

AND

Cushions.

If you are in the market kindly call, we can make it interesting for you in quality and at prices sufficient to induce you to buy.

PADGITT BROS.,

248 & 250 COMMERCE ST., DALLAS, TEXAS.

A Reverie.

WHEN a man contemplates giving up his home, with all its sacred surroundings, in anticipation of removal to a distant state, he may well pause and ask himself, "What of the new country," from which such favorable reports have come. The weight of a great responsibility seems to oppress him for what he says to himself: If another error is made, it will certainly prove irretrieveable. The last move was a poor one, for the soil here is too thin; the winters too long and rigorous, and the summers too uncertain. There is too much wind, rain, ice and snow, and too little sunshine.

Yet one may go farther and fare worse. Well that old saying has puzzled many a wiser brain than mine and often turned aside far greater resolutions. Yet I must go; I have determined upon that, but whither?

California is too far away and land there is too costly, and as one must irrigate, he must constantly pay taxes on irrigation ditches and I know nothing of that method of agriculture, and yet, I would seek a country which is in many respects like that which I hear of California.

At the click of the gate the dreamer awakens from his reverie to receive the morning mail What is this? A Souvenir Guide of Dallas, the metropolis of the Lone Star Empire State.

Is this the land of which I have been dreaming? He reads on and on about the land that has fewer drawbacks than any other that can

be named; a land which has an assured future, where industry and good management prevail; a land of salubrious clime and unequalled soil, capable of producing the cereals of the Northern and Middle states, and the luscious fruits of the semi-tropics, where the figs of Persia grow side by side, in the open air, with the hardier fruits of Northern climes.; a land exempt from earthquakes, and blizzards, and ice and snow—a very paradise for cattle, and horses, sheep, and swine and poultry—a land in which the laws protect the homestead and daily wages, for the shelter and maintainance of the wife and little ones; truly the vertible promised Canan Land of milk and honey, which Moses first viewed from Sinai's crest.

After the days of preparation, and a few hours rapid gliding behind the iron horse, the dreamer reaches the anticipated home.

Amazed, he beholds, not only the promised wonders in soil and clime, but, instead of the dreary and lonely prairie and the cheerless and rugged frontier home—a landscape beauteous with thrifty farms, and luxuriant crops, and lordly oaks, and graceful elms, lovely shrubs and flowers, singing birds and honey bees, such as the frigid North never produced; netted with railways, telegraph and telephone lines; dotted with school buildings and church edifices, mills and factories; refreshed with flowing springs, and artesian wells, and navig'ble streams, and abundant rains in season; and above all, the *City of Dallas* near by, with its tall spires and smoking factories, mammoth stores and beautiful homes, where the shrill whistle of the steamers Harvey and Dallas, fortells of that halcyon time, when the metropolis shall send her products, at water rates, to the seaboard and the world.

THE SECURITY
MORTGAGE AND TRUST CO.

DALLAS, TEXAS.

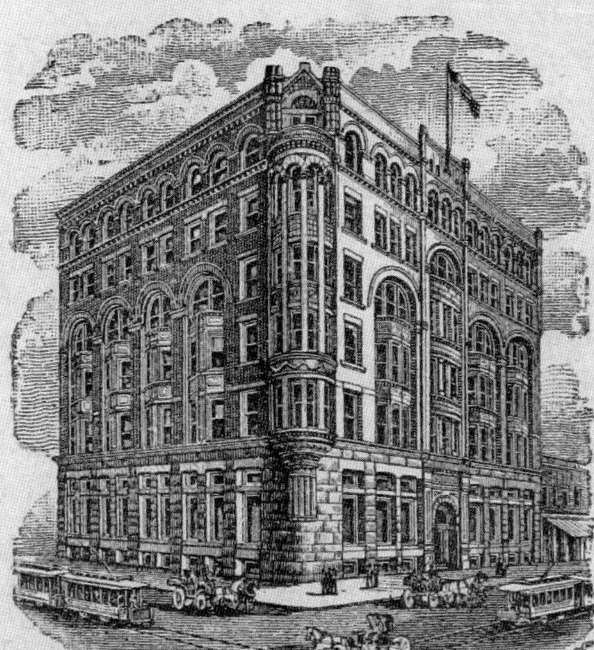

PAID UP CAPITAL $500,000.

OFFICERS:

J. T. Trezevant,
Presiaent

J. C. O'Connor,
1st. Vice-President

A. R. Andrews,
2nd Vice-President.

H. A. Kahler,
3rd Vice-Pres. & Gen'l Mgr.

Wm. G. Breg,
Secretary.

De Edward Greer,
Attorney & Trust Officer.

LOANS MONEY on Improved Farms in the Black Belt of Texas, and on First-Class City Property in the larger cities of Texas.

DALLAS.

IN THE poet's view, dreams are visitors from the ivory gate, or children of an idle brain, but science is more prosaic, and teaches that dreams may be realities. In history we have many iridescent dreamers; in fact, all our great men have been such, and in many instances the dream has surpassed all human expectations. Little did the young lawyer, John Neely Bryan, as he he pitched his lonely tent on the banks of the Trinity river in 1840, dream that he was the founder of a city which was to be the future metropolis of the South.

Wonderful has been the growth and unparalelled the expansion of this whole Republic within the last decade, but no section has ever seen such wonderful development as has enterprising Dallas.

In 1870 the population was only 1700; but fortunately for Dallas, the accursed spirit of division, which has blighted the fair prospects of many a young city, was unknown here.

Great enterprises and boundless public spirit were stamped on every feature of the city. Enterprise and industry have achieved results as startling as the wave of the magician's wand, and in this atom of time has sprung up, as if it were by magic, a city with a population of 61,855 souls. Nor has the march of development slackened, but the watch-word is still "Onward!" and Dallas is ranked among the largest and most progressive cities of the South.

If you knew Dallas ten or fifteen years ago and should depend upon your memory for a

picture of the Dallas of to-day, you have a very small idea of the character of the future metropolis of the South. Such changes as have taken place: Stately churches, magnificent business blocks, towering office buildings, huge mercantile and manufacturing establishments, and many beautiful homes.

Dallas has an ideal site for a city. It being over 500 feet above the sea level, one constantly catches picturesque views of the surrounding country,from its broad and well kept thoroughfares.

In 1872, the first railroad, the Houston & Texas Central, reached Dallas; then came the Texas & Pacific, the Dallas & Wichita (now of the M. K. & T. system), the Gulf, Colorado & Santa Fe, the Trunk. and the Missouri, Kansas & Texas, giving six railways, thus making connections in twelve different direction. These roads have done more for the progress and development of the city, than any other factor in its history.

The track of the Chicago, Rock Island & Pacific is now completed as far as Fort Worth, which leaves only a few miles yet to be laid, before her engines will be steaming into the Texas metropolis. The Cotton Belt (St. Louis Southwestern), is also making preparations to extend is line into the city, and these two lines will be added to the system of railways centering in Dallas. In fact, such transportation facilities are the only basis for the solid, substantial growth of the city, and, on the other hand, a city that possesses such facilities is

bound to go ahead. Such has been the experience of every ambitious city.

As a manufacturing and industrial center, Dallas presents superior advantages. Its geographical location will soon be able to give it a water route, via. the Trinity river, to the sea, thus affording her greater facilities for the transportation of her poducts, than any other section in the great Southwest. While Dallas possesses more manufacturing establishments than most cities of the same size, it is, in this field of development, particularly, that capital seeking investment, can reap the richest har vest. Dallas now has 183 manufacturies, and still has ample room for more. And, with the development of the now idle prairie, she will build factories and enterprising industries. Doubtless there is more money made in the manufacturing business, than any other business engaged in, in this state, with an equal amount of capital. To all manufacturers wishing to change their location, Dallas offers a field unsurpassed both in matters of its nat ural resources and shipping facilities. She wants no adventurers, but to factory men, who are the promoters of legitimate schemes,a warm welcome is extended. She has a field for factories of almost any kind, and any one will do well to investigate before locating elsewhere.

The Texas State Fair Association and grounds, situated at Dallas, are the pride and admiration, of not only the stock growers of Dallas and vicinity, but of this whole state, and the interest now being manifested gives

assurance that the coming fair will be crowned with greater success than any of its predecessors.

The water supply is undoubtedly the best of any city in Texas. Besides the water system, which is supplied from the Trinity river, costing $1,500.000, with a pumping capacity of 27,000,000 gallons per day: there are thirty-seven artesian wells, owned by the city and private parties These wells give a never failing supply of sweet, pure water, with a capacity of from 5000 to 10,000 gallons per hour.

The city is well lighted by electricity and gas and it is claimed that Dallas is one of the best lighted cities in the state. There are over 300 arc lights and 4500 incandescent lamps. There are also several private plants for various purposes and light for business houses and private residences.

Dallas has thirty miles of paved and macadamized streets, well kept; and forty-nine miles of street railway, furnishing excellent transportation to all parts of the city.

Dallas boasts of one of the best equipped and most serviceable paid fire departments in the country. The latest improved Gamewell fire alarm, with sixty-one boxes and 190 hydrants, is in use.

Among the public buildings of which the citizens are justly proud, is the courthouse, which is a magnificent structure. It was erected at a cost of $350,000. The view from the dome is simply superb, covering the heart of the busy city, and the pretty Trinity river, with its green banks, and the net-work of rail-

Wm. B. Robinson. Marshall Bird. H. W. Robinson.

ROBINSON, BIRD & CO.,

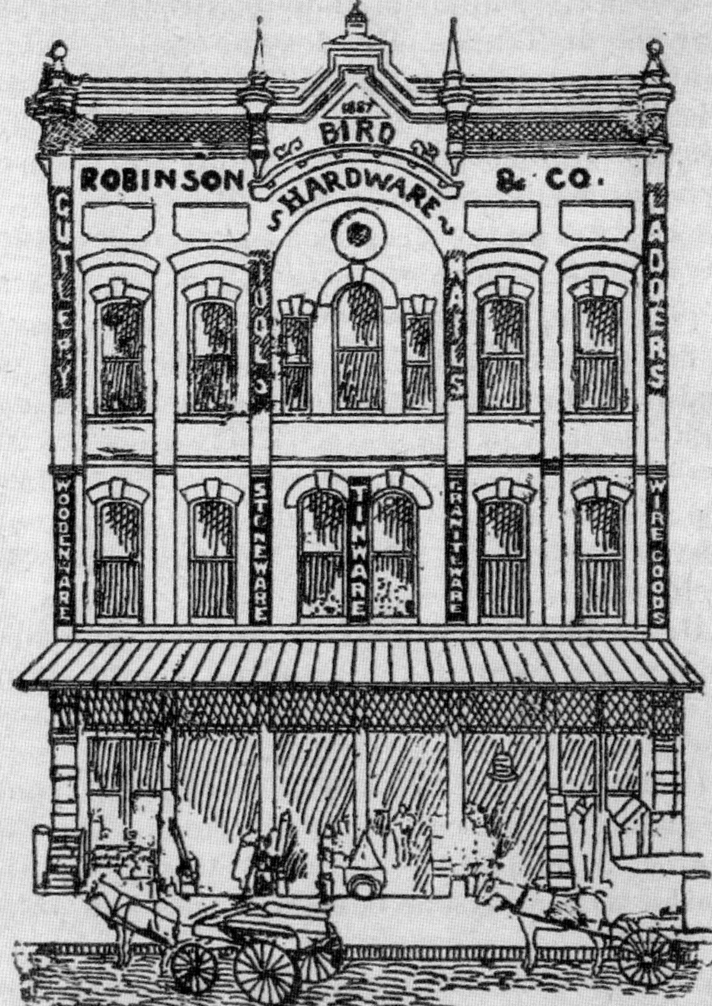

WHOLESALE AND RETAIL

HARDWARE, STOVES AND TINWARE,

HOUSE FURNISHING GOODS A SPECIALTY.

308 & 310 ELM ST., *Telephone 571.* **DALLAS, TEXAS.**

roads. Visitors should not fall to see this view. Other beautiful buildings are the city hall, costing $100,000; the United States post-office and custom house, costing $255,000. and the commodious stone opera house. Besides these are many more fine public buildings, which were erected without regard to expense, which goes to show that Dallas is a wide awake city. There are forty-six church edifices, of which many are stately and grand, and which represent all the different denominations.

The educational facilities are of the highest order, and evince the highly cultivated character of Dallas people. There are fourteen public schools, eighteen private schools, business colleges, and convents; schools of design, music halls, etc. This is a consideration of vast importance to heads of families, engaged in any industry or profession and desiring to combine their material progress with the highest possible good for their children. There is no city in the South blessed with the educational advantages of Dallas.

Another indication of the intellectual wellfare of the city is the hearty endorsement and support given the press. The Dallas News, an eight-page seven-column paper, (enlarging its Sunday issue to twenty pages), is without its equal in the South. It can be safely asserted that the "News" is the most popular paper in Texas. Its circulation is ten to one of any other daily. It is the only paper in the South which runs its own special trains, giving the news of the world to points within one hundred miles before breakfast.

The Times-Herald, also an eight-page, evening paper, has no superior in any city of this size.

The Texas Farm and Ranch is the largest and most extensively circulated paper of its kind in the Southwest. Besides these, there are twenty-six other flourishing newspapers, and several magazines.

Dallas has five national and several private banks, that are reliable and enjoying unlimited public confidence, and which have a capital and surplus of $4,000,000. These banks are as solid financial institutions as can be found in the South.

There are also several local building societies and strong national associations, with an authorized capital of $200,000,000.

As a wholesale center Dallas takes the lead and occupies the field, and will always control the jobbing trade of the Southwest, as she has secured reasonable freight rates, and now invites not only Texas, but also other states to come and do a jobbing trade. In Dallas are located wholesale houses of nearly all classes of business; in fact, anything that can be carried in job lots. One striking illustration of the magnitude of the city's trade is given in one item of agricultural implements and machinery; reaching as it does over $10,000,000 annually, being second to only one other city in the United States in this branch of business, Kansas City. It is estimated that during the past year the following wholesale business was done in Dallas:

Machinery and Electric Supplies	$10.000.000
Dry Goods, etc.	9.000.000
Boots and Shoes	1.250.000
Drugs	1.000.000
Agricultural Implements	7.000,000
Jewelry	600.000
Sewing Machines	250.000
Furniture	650.000

And in all branches of business in like proportion.

During the past ten years Dallas has been making rapid strides, so that to-day its wonderful progress is perceptable on all sides. "In all the North and East there is not another city like Dallas, with so large an area of rich and productive lands tributary to it, which has not a population of 150,000 to 500,000. Many of the Northern and Eastern cities are not more than two hundred miles apart; yet Dallas is six hundred miles south of Kansas City, eight hundred miles southwest of St. Louis, four hundred miles west of Memphis and five hundred miles from New Orleans, most admirably located, with a territory extending four hundred miles west, three hundred miles south, two hundred miles east and one hundred miles north—an empire within itself—with Dallas its commercial center."

The growth of Dallas has been rapid, but permanent. This progress has been the result of the systematic and energetic use of the advantages which nature has bestowed, coupled with the energy of enthusiasm and determination.

It is a remarkably healthy city, and no serious epidemic has ever visited it. The death rate is very low, being only ten to the thousand.

A Wrought Iron, Hand-Made Buggy.

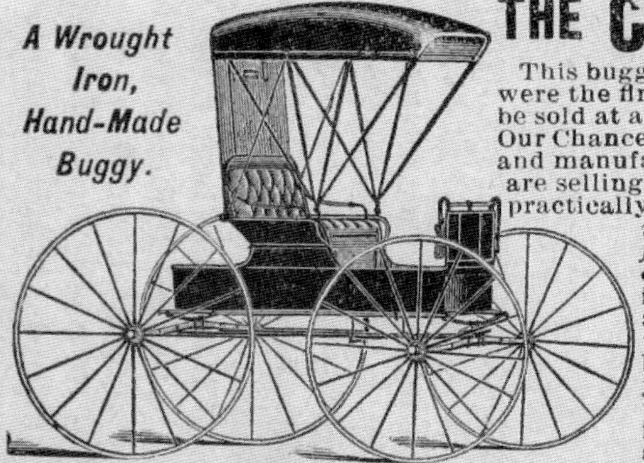

THE CHANCELLOR BREWSTER BUGGY.

This buggy has for years been a specialty with us, in fact, we were the first introducers of a full trimmed buggy that could be sold at a moderate price; its success has been phenomenal. Our Chancellor buggy has been imitated by nearly every jobber and manufacturer in the country, but the fact remains that we are selling the best buggy ever put up for the money. It is practically a wrought iron *hand made* buggy, the *axle clips, reach irons, top joints and solid shifting rails are forged out by hand from the best Norway Iron.* **Our competitors are using malleable and cast iron,** still they will tell you theirs is "just as good as the Chancellor." They know it's false, and time will so demonstrate it. It has full Leather top and back curtain, rubber side curtains, silver plated top joints, dash-rail, hub-bands, hand-holds and curtain fasteners on back curtain, and is absolutely reliable in every way and the best ever sold for the price we ask. Ask your dealer for **P. O. Co.'s Chancellor** and take no substitute. See that our name-plate is on the back. Write us if you can't get it from him. **Over 1000 vehicles constantly in stock.** *Send for beautiful Illustrated Catalogue, free.* We also carry full line of **Mowers, Hay Rakes, Hay Presses, Balingties, Threshers, Traction Engines, Sorghum Mills and Evaporators, Binder Twine, Corn Shellers, Grain Drills, Harness. Write us for your wants. Largest and best Equipped Implement House in the South.** PARLIN & ORENDORFF CO., DALLAS, TEX

The society in this section is excellent. The people are anxious for emmigration, and will bestow a hearty welcome.

Fortune knocks once at every man's door. At this moment, kind reader, she may be "tapping, gently tapping," at your door. Will you heed the summons and improve the golden opportunity to provide for the future, or permit her to pass on and bequeath the inheritance to your more wide-awake and responsive neighbor? Do not delay. Remember that,

"Procrastination is the Thief of Time.
Make good the present and Success is Thine."

Oak Cliff, Suburb of the City of Dallas

THE worshipper of Nature here may find, "A rich repast where he may feast the mind."

Could he who, in the plaintive story of "Evangeline," sung of the beautiful "Teche country," to-day visit the beautiful Oak Cliff addition, he would find so much of the practical and attractive, joined with the picturesque, that he would bid his muse begone. Here where the flowers kissed the morning dew, and the primeval forests echoed only with the songs of native warblers, has been made to-day one of the most beautiful residence additions to the thriving and charming metropolis of Texas.

This beautiful tract of land is on a high plateau. Oak Cliff is recognized as the residence seekers, sequestered spot. It has its own electric light and water plants. It also has a fine school system, and it points with pride to

its magnificent college for the higher education of young women.

It is four stories high, and in the matter of appointments and furnishings it is unsurpassed by any other college boarding home in the United States.

The College can accomodate six hundred pupils.

The Dallas and Oak Cliff Elevated Railroad (with its principal station corner of Jefferson and Commerce streets, on Court House Square) substantially constructed and elevated above the flood tide of the Trinity river, which it crosses—forms a belt of ten miles from the business center of Dallas, re-entering the city from a westerly direction, on Main street. The system which dominates the management of this road involves the strictest discipline among employees. and the most rigid exactitude in every detail. Trains leave promptly and run on schedule time. The fare is only five cents—the same as on street cars.

A contract has been let for a Motor line extending from Oak Cliff to the fair grounds in east Dallas, the distance of nine miles.

A two minutes walk from the station, along Park street, fringed on both sides with beautiful shade trees, brings you to the auditorium, where is found an amphitheatre with capacity to seat 2000, and equipments that would do credit to a large city.

J. B. ADOUE, President. **J. D. ESTES, Cashier.**

THE

National Bank of Commerce,

CAPITAL - - - $150,000.

DALLAS, TEXAS.

DIRECTORS:

JAMES MORONEY, .	Moroney Hardware Co.
J. M. HARRY, .	Brick Manufacturer.
T. W. GRIFFITHS, .	Lumber Dealer.
F. G. MOORE, .	Moore & Rawlins, Sash, Doors, &c
R. E. L. KNIGHT, .	Attorney at Law.
C. A. ROBERTSON, .	Machinery and Implements.
J. B. ADOUE, .	President.
S. J. HOWELL .	Boots and Shoes.

J. L. TICHENOR,

DENTIST.

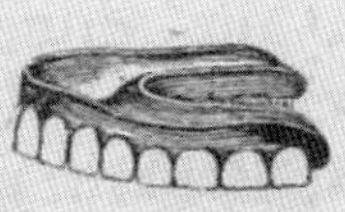

Amalgam Fillings - - - $1.00

Teeth Extracted - - - - 50

Treatment and Filling of Dead and

Diseased Teeth a Specialty.

ALL WORK GUARANTEED

569 ELM STREET, Cor. H. & T. C. R. R.

DALLAS, TEXAS.

Just adjacent and spreading from the auditorium, is the Oak Cliff Park, which occupies an area of 125 acres of natural beauty, improved here and there with trees and flowers, diversified by hill and dale. It is penetrated in all directions by beautiful and well-kept drives. This park is kept free from all objectionable features. The Park is bordered on the south by a beautiful lake, half a mile in length and 200 yards in width.

It is the design of the projectors, and the citizens of Oak Cliff, to encourage and secure the location in Oak Cliff of desireable citizens only; and with that purpose constantly in view they have employed such safeguards and expedients as they command, and as a result of this policy Oak Cliff contains a distinctly moral people. Intoxicating liquors cannot be found within her limits. In keeping with this policy, no sort of questionable resorts are tolerated

On the whole, Oak Cliff is at present a thorough-going and hustling town, with flattering promises of continued and assured success.

DALLAS COUNTY.

WHEN we consider the location of Dallas County, in the heart of the wealthiest and most productive portion of the state, where, for a radius of from 100 to 300 miles, it is surrounded by as fine a farming country as can be found on the face of the globe, settled by an industrious and enterprising class of citizens, and penetrated by a net work of railroads, we need not wonder at its marvelous growth. No county can show greater advancement than Dallas, the "Banner County" of Texas. Hundreds, yea thousands, of her broad acres, o'er which cattle and horses roamed and grazed unmolested not more than a quarter of a century ago, have been converted into great blooming gardens, and now shoot forth into the hand of industry, as if touched by a magic wand, the products of untold happiness and wealth.

The baleful and mournful cry of the coyote has long since been hushed. and, in its place, comes the far away bellowing of the pensive cow, the bleating of the sheep and the barking of the farmer's dog.

The prairie trail has been supplanted by the well kept country road, dotted on either side by the pretty home of the thrifty farmer. The slow ox train has given way to the iron horse and railroads are running hither and yon past

beautiful farms and through charming thrifty, little towns and cities, and electric lights flash out on the evening air in place of the coon hunter's torch. In brief, upon a beautiful landscape a picture of highly attained civilization has been and is being painted. Thrift and enterprise, brain and capital are grappling with the wealth of field and forrest and making of Dallas County the garden spot of the South.

The county is watered by the Trinity river and its tributaries, which supply an abundance of water for stock during the entire year. Besides these there are a large number of running streams and natural springs and artesian wells making the water supply in this county unquestionably the best and most abundant of any section in this portion of the state.

The lands in Dallas county are probably more varied in quality than any other part of the state of equal area, and in consequence are adapted to a greater variety of crops. There is the black-waxy prairie, the light-gray sandy land, the black-sandy loam and the rich alluvium of the bottoms; each especially adapted to special crops, each presenting its advantages, and all yielding rich returns to the hand of industry.

The surface is beautifully undulating, thoroughly drained and in consequence is, to a great extent, free from those distressing malarial diseases so dreaded by home seekers in the South. The gulf breezes blow during the greater part of the year, and no one could help being impressed with a climate so mild, invig-

orating and healthful, where the sun's heat is softened by the gulf breeze to such an extent that the longest summer days rarely become oppressive and one never fails to enjoy a good night's rest. The winters are mild, the themometer scarcely going as low as zero, and when visited by cold weather the duration is never more than two or three days; thereby allowing out door work to be prosecuted almost the whole year round.

Dallas county ranks first in population. Some people say: "Yes; I know that Dallas county is capable of sustaining a very dense population; but I prefer more elbow room." Well, perhaps that question has two sides; but here are some of the advantages of living in a thickly settled country: Land purchased now from $15 to $25 per acre will inhance in value to $75 and $100 per acre, and even higher as time goes on. The cities and towns will grow steadily, and all sorts of manufacturing enterprises will spring up, for such masses of people will make ready home markets, and supply an abundance of labor. Schools and Colleges will flourish; more railroads will be built to transact the business of the teeming thousands of people. The farms will be small and cultivated like gardens, while all the best ideas in agriculture and stock raising will prevail. Churches and literary societies will be numerous; there will be very few rich people,

J. F. THOMAS,

Real Estate AND Collecting Agent,

484 ELM ST., DALLAS, TEX.

H. C. Darwin. E. R. E. Witte.

WITTE & DARWIN,

Manufacturers and Dealers in

SADDLES AND HARNESS,

479 ELM ST., DALLAS, TEX.

Repairing Harness, and Trimming and Painting Buggies are Our Specialties.

All Work Hand-Made and Satisfaction Guaranteed.

Cheapest Place in The City.

TRINITY DRUG STORE,

R. F. EISENLOHR, Prescriptionist

The Oldest Druggist in Dallas.

384 ELM ST., near Ervay. Telephone 453.

and very few poor ones; the aggregate wealth will be immense; taxes will be low and public improvements the best, charities will increase in munificence as even now, the blind, the insane and infirm are well cared for. In short, civilization will attain the highest development, and no land under the sun will contain a better or happier people. This is no fancy sketch, but a faint outline of what is in store for this section of Texas. That all this and more will be realized is just as certain as that peace and good government shall continue to bless this wonderful country.

We doubt whether an investment in farm lands in the old states would pay even six per cent. on the money. We do not believe an investor in the lands in the old states would make much by an increase in values. In Dallas county the values of lands have doubled themselves every few years, and when put in cultivation will net thirty to forty per cent. annually on the investment. Is there anything better than such land anywhere?

To the denizens of the frozen Northwest this would prove another Canan, a land where the sun never ceases to shine; where the freezing blasts are tempered by the mild breath of the gulf stream; where the plowman's song may be heard throughout the year, and generous nature never tires of giving good gifts to the hand of industry, where a generous soil only awaits the hand of the husbandman to smile with plenty, and where the iron hand of winter never falls

The social status of the people of this county is equal to that of any other section of the

Union. Their houses are good and well-kept and in many cases luxurious. Their farms are well stocked, well fenced and intelligently cultivated. All the comforts and conveniences of life are at command and enjoyed by all. The most improved farm implements and machinery are in general use and there is not probably ten acres in the county where a sulky plow or cultivator could not be used.

There is the strictest observance of order and law, and crime is probably as great a stranger in Dallas county as in the most cultivated societies of the older states. The people are hospitable, generous and sociable, kind and obliging to strangers, always willing to assist or advise. The mass of people are comfortably off and live well. Poverty, such as is common in almost all older communities, is unknown, and discord is a stranger.

We no longer have whole states from which to select a location for a home. As the increase of population continues, new homes are in constant demand. Why remain in a location giving small returns when here one-half the labor now performed would bring a much greater income?

Dallas county extends no welcome to idlers, rich or poor. But for industry or integrity, for capital of cash, for capital of brains or capital of brawn there is an abundance of possibilities. Dallas County has to offer rich lands at nominal prices, mild climate, excellent health, numerous churches, free schools, productive soil, good markets, plenty of grass and water, low taxes and excellent railroad facilities. These are facts; and we invite investigation and extend a hearty welcome.

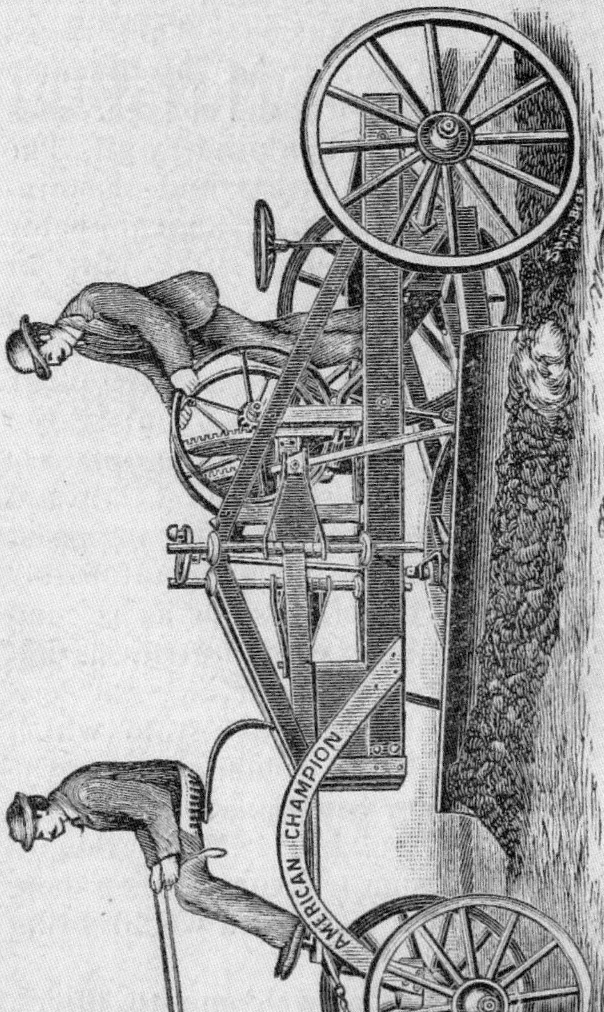
AMERICAN CHAMPION

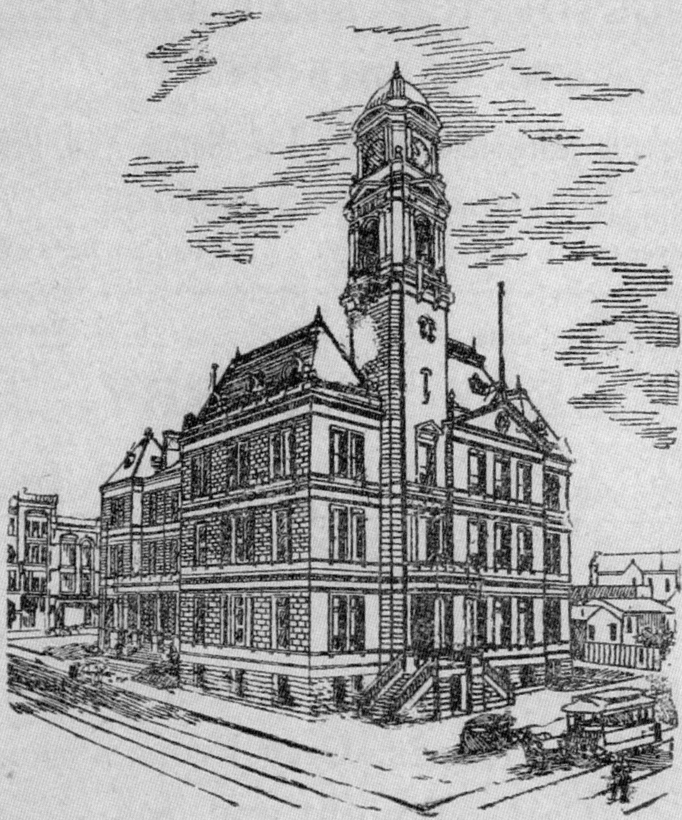

✦ Dallas Post-Office, ✦

COSTING $255,000.

WM. M. C. HILL, POSTMASTER.

CLERKS.

Alpha Willey............Assistant Postmaster
Albert G. Joyce...............Financial Clerk
M. F. Sterett........... .....Chief M. O. Clerk
John B. Miller..............Ass't M. O. Clerk
M. J. Marshall.............Third M. O. Clerk
H. M. Price..............Chief Mailing Clerk

B. D. Taylor..............Paper Mailing Clerk
Grant G. Campbell..............Mailing Clerk
J. H. Robertson..................Mailing Clerk
Richard Griffin..................Mailing Clerk
A. M. Baker.......................Mailing Clerk
Fred L. Sawyer ....Stamper
S. J. Marshall..Supt. of Carriers and Chf. Dis.
J. M. Bolin.....Enquiry Clerk and Distributor
Geo. C. Young......Box Clerk and Distributor
Benj. Wilmut, Jr............Night Distributor
Thos. H. Watson.........Chief Registry Clerk
W. M. Cochran...........Ass't Registry Clerk
Rachael E. Miller................Stamp Clerk
G. W. Barkley..............Forwarding Clerk
S. D. Lindsey..........General Delivery Clerk
H. C. Buel.............General Delivery Clerk

CARRIERS.

S. P. Bowen, Edward Munckton,
Jas. H. Evans, H. P. Nichols,
J. E. Hess, Alfred Rockhold,
Sam Hiltpold, J. K. Withers,
J. H. Jackson, D. D. Daugherty,
Robt. McCormick, Wm. W. Farley,
Ben H. Hill, Wm. R. Hughes,
J. B. Leamon, A. C. Wells,
Thos. H. Nesmith, Irving Purnell,
G. W. E. Merewether.

SUBSTITUTE CARRIERS.

Geo. W. Cruise..C. J. Castle..Jos. V. Danner.

TOTAL NUMBER OF EMPLOYES.

Clerks..................................	22
Carriers................................	19
Substitute Carriers......................	3
Total..................................	44

Five more carriers will be added to the list September 1, 1894.—Two more clerks.

TRAVEL IN COMFORT

By Taking Advantage of the

Superior ✦ Train ✦ Service,

Elegant Equipment and Fast Time

—VIA THE—

THE SHORT LINE TO

NEW ORLEANS, MEMPHIS,

AND POINTS IN THE

SOUTHEAST.

TAKE "THE ST. LOUIS LIMITED,"

12 HOURS SAVED

BETWEEN

TEXAS AND ST LOUIS!

THE DIRECT LINE TO ALL POINTS IN

MEXICO, NEW MEXICO, ARIZONA, OREGON and CALIFORNIA.

Pullman Palace Sleeping Cars

—TO—

ST. LOUIS, LITTLE ROCK, SHREVEPORT, NEW ORLEANS, DENVER, EL PASO, LOS ANGELES & SAN FRANCISCO.

For rates, tickets and all information apply to or address any of the ticket agents or

W. A. DASHIELL, Trav. Pass. Agent.
GASTON MESLIER, Gen'l Pass. & Tk't Ag't.
L. S. THORNE, 3d. Vice-Pres't. Gen'l Mangr.
DALLAS, TEXAS.

STATEMENT

Of Business Transacted at the Post-Office in Dallas, for year ending June, 1894.

RECEIPTS.

Sales at Stamp Window	$ 98,069.98
Sales of Special Request Envelopes	12,426.60
Postage Rec'd for 2d Class Matter	8,735.81
Cash Rec'd for Box Rents	2,239.25
Cash Rec'd for Waste Paper	10.81
Cash Rec'd for Old Furniture	1 00
Total	$121,483.45

DISBURSMENTS.

Postmaster's Salary	$ 3,400.00
Post-Office Clerks' Salaries	18,256.00
Railway Postal Clerks Salary	2,900.00
Am't paid Spec'l Delivery Messeng'rs	347.44
Letter Carriers' Salaries	15,837.50
Incidental expenses Carrier Service	2,024.74
Expense of Canceling Machine.	294.81
Miscellaneous Expenses	29.42
Credit Allowed for Redeemed Stock Returned Department	273.22
Credit on Dead Letter Bills	29.42
Surplus Remitted Ass't Treasurer at at New Orleans	78,113.04
Total	121,483.45

Receipts, 1894	$121,483.45
Receipts, 1893	120,251.11
Increase	1,232.34

MONEY ORDERS ISSUED 1894.

		Amount.
16,961	Money Orders issued	$182,246.74
8,228	Postal Notes issued	12,794.50
838	Intern'l Money Orders issued,	13,491 01
25,027	Total	208,632.25

MONEY ORDERS PAID 1894.

		Amount.
63,788	Money Orders paid	$676,732.30
28,518	Postal Notes paid	43,260.59
113	Intern'l Money Orders paid	2,458.98
92,419	Total	722,451.87

This shows an increase in the number of Money Orders of 1,387 and in value of $26,010.53 over the year 1893.

In Money Orders Paid the increase in number is 16,608, and in value increase $101,150.36.

STREET LETTER BOXES IN USE.

Large Boxes	20
Small Boxes	94
Mail Chutes	2
Total	116
Stamp Agencies	3

OFFICE HOURS.

Money Order Dept	9 a. m. to 5 p. m.
Registry Dept	9 a. m. to 6 p. m.
Stamp Window	8 a. m. to 6 p. m.
Sundays	10 a. m. to 11 a. m.
General Delivery	8 a. m, to 7 p. m.
Sundays	9 a. m. to 11 a. m.

OAK CLIFF POST-OFFICE.

Arrivals and Departures of Mails at Oak Cliff, Texas.

Arrives	7:00 a. m.	Leaves 5:30 a. m.
"	10:40 a. m.	" 9:00 a. m.
"	4:40 p. m.	" 3:30 p. m.

OFFICE HOURS.

Week Days	7:00 a. m. to 6:30 p. m.
Sundays	9:00 a. m. to 10:00 a. m.

W. M. Ward, P. M.
L. M. Martin, Asst. P. M.
M. A. Posten, Clerk.
C. M. Jones, Mail Messenger.

OZONA

is the County Seat of

CROCKETT COUNTY,

TEXAS

and derives its name by suggestion from the
salubrious and health giving climate
of that whole region.

THIS OZONA COUNTRY

is one of the finest portions of our State,

Fine Soil, Fine Water and Fine Grass.

FOR CHEAP LANDS AND RANCHES

in this section, or for town lots at Ozona
where there are very fine school
facilities and good society,

write to **E. M. POWELL.**

401 Main St., Dallas, Texas.

No trouble to answer questions. opposite Postoffice.

RATES OF POSTAGE.

Letter rates of postage, 2 cents for each ounce or fraction thereof, throughout United States, Mexico and Canada.

Newspapers, periodicals, 1 cent for four ounces; books, photographs, etc., 1 cent for two ounces or fraction thereof.

Merchandise and other printed matter, 1 cent for each 1 ounce or fraction thereof.

Letters registered 8 cents, in addition to postage.

Money Orders for sums not exceeding $100 issued; fee 3 to 30 cents.

International Money Orders issued for sums not exceeding $100; fee 10 cents to $100.

The Texas & Pacfiic Railway.

By reason of its mileage and location in the State. The Texas & Pacific Railway is the most important of all railway lines in Texas. Its entire length is 1499 miles, of which 1125 are in Texas. and 357 are in Louisiana,. In addition to its railway mileage it also operates a steamboat line between Shreveport, La. and Alexander, La., a distance of 300 miles. The main line extending from Texarkana to El Paso. via. Marshall and Dallas, has a length of 969 miles; the Trans-Continental division, from Texarkana to Fort Worth, via. Sherman, has a length of 244 miles; and the New Orleans division, extending from New Orleans, La. to Marshall, Texas has a length of 374, miles. With its connections, it forms one of the most important thoroughfares between the Gulf States and the Upper Mississippi Valley. between the Atlantic Coast and the Pacific Coast, and between Mexico and the entire North and East. Crossing the state from East to West it connects with almost every important railway line in Texas, and all points in Mexico, New Mexico and Louisiana can be reached by way of the Texas & Pacific.

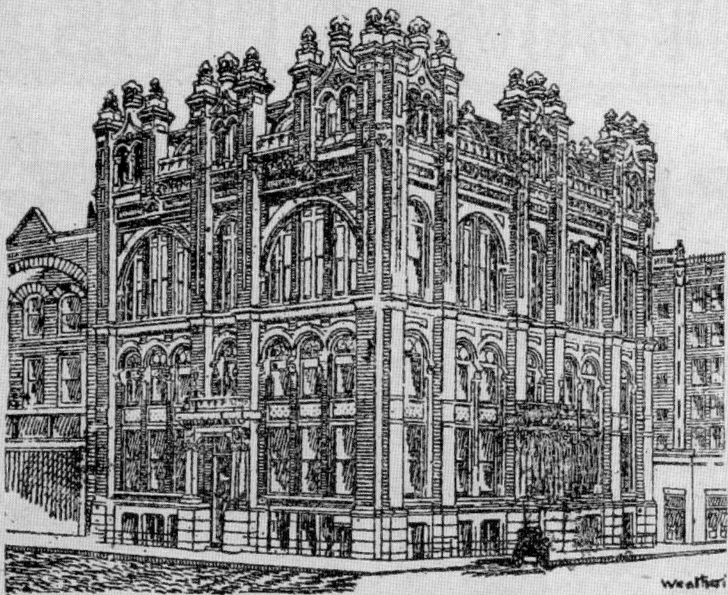

CITY GOVERNMENT.

CITY HALL, COR. COMMERCE AND AKARD.

Mayor...... ....Bryan T. Barry
Mayor, *pro tem*........ ....C. A. Cour
City Attorney........... ....A. P. Wozencraft
Auditor.................... ....J. F. Caldwell
Secretary ....C. G Morgan
Assessor...Ben Melton
Treasurer...................... ....E. M. Reardon
Judge.......... ....Kenneth Foree
Clerk City Court......... ....M. Kahn
Chief Police................ ....J. C. Arnold
Asst. Chief Police............... ....G. E. Cornwall
City Tax Collector.... .... Tom Scott
Engineer............. ....R. W. Havens
Supt. Water Works........................ J. M. Stróng
Health Officer................... ....V. P. Armstrong
Chemist ....L. M. Conner
Chief Fire Department........... . ...T. Wilkinson
Street Supt...................................H. P. Golden
Electrician......................................W. A. Fraser

ALDERMEN.

1st Ward—	P. O'Keefe,	2nd Ward—	A. M. Cochran,
3rd "	C. P. Smith.	4th "	Chas. Kahn,
5th "	Frank Kelley,	6th "	M. J. P Lacy,
7th "	C. A. Cour,	8th "	D. R. Long,
9th "	J.C.Woodside,	10th "	Jno. C. Corder,
11th "	C. E. Bird,	12th "	J. R. Briggs,

FINANCIAL CONDITION.

Bonded Debt.......................................$2,014,500
Assessed value Property, Jan. 1. 1893..............23,131,600
Assessed value Property, Jan. 1, 1894, estimated, 20,000,000
Floating Debt. none.
Tax Rate, 1894, 1 9-20 per cent.

VALUE CITY PROPERTY.

Water Works	$1,009,000
Public Schools	292,000
City Hospital	22,000
Engine Houses and other Property	177,000
Thirty miles paved streets	703,000
Twenty-seven miles sewerage	305,000
Three Artesian wells	22,000
Total,	$2,530,000

Estimated Population. 62,000.

FIRE DEPARTMENT.

The Fire Department has four steam engines, two Chemical Engines, five Hose Carriages, 1 Aerial Truck, one City Truck. Chief and full force to manage the Department.

POLICE DEPARTMENT.

The Police Department has Chief of Police, Assistant Chief, thirty-five policemen and three detectives.

WATER WORKS.

The City Water Works have 58 miles of mains, 438 fire hydrants; the water privileges bringing in a revenue of $87,000 per annum Amount of water pumped during last fiscal year, 2,879,703,477 gallons; amount pumped into the mains, 1,496,438,983 gallons, a daily consumption of 4,100,000. The daily pumping capacity of the plant, 26,500,000 gallons. Capacity of reservoirs, 135,000,000 gallons.

Steamer Harvey, of Dallas.

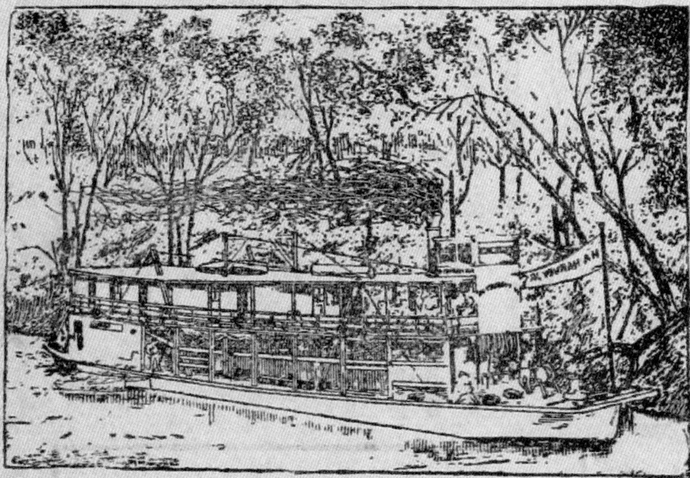

The Trinity River.

"Men may come and Men may go,
But I go on Forever."

MANY are the records which prove that the Trinity River was navigable from Trinity Bay and the Gulf up to within some eighty miles from Dallas, and particularly until the Houston & Texas Central railroad was built between Houston and Dallas. These records are dated only a few years back and many of the captains, pilots and hands of the steamboats which used to ply on this river, also many shippers are still living, all of whom we have lately heard report that these steamboats used to carry as many as 1000 bales of cotton down to the Gulf ports, particularly Galveston. Hence in this instance, as in so many others we might mention, railroads

"killed, or rather "stunned" navigation, and, as was the case elsewhere, so here also, navigation is coming to life again and it will do so with a vengence, too. The Dallas people, as those of other towns before them, have found out that no city could become great that had not at its disposal water and rail facilities for their freight. The advantages of a water highway to the seaboard are many fold. Other cities in America and Europe have particularly found out that; by the fact that they could enjoy this double mode of transportation they secured much lower rates which caused them a great increase in trafic and manufacturers.

It was also found out that that rivers were not detrimental to railroads, because heavy raw material would have remained untouched on the rivers banks, manufactured there and shipped as manufactured articles by the railroads. Hence rivers are now said to be the "natural feeders of freight" to iron roads.

No sooner were the Dallas people convinced of these facts than not content with their twelve spokes of railroads, they determined to convert the "dirty little Trinity river," as they called it, of rafts and snags, of boughs and other obstructions, into an open waterway to the sea. This done, they had a steamboat 120 feet long by 20' beam, to run up to Dallas. They damed and locked the Trinity and they will continue these improvements for a year or two at most when the Trinity river will be permanently open to navigation from Dallas to the Gulf.

On the very day this navigation is secured will dawn for Dallas a new era of prosperity that will have but few parallels.

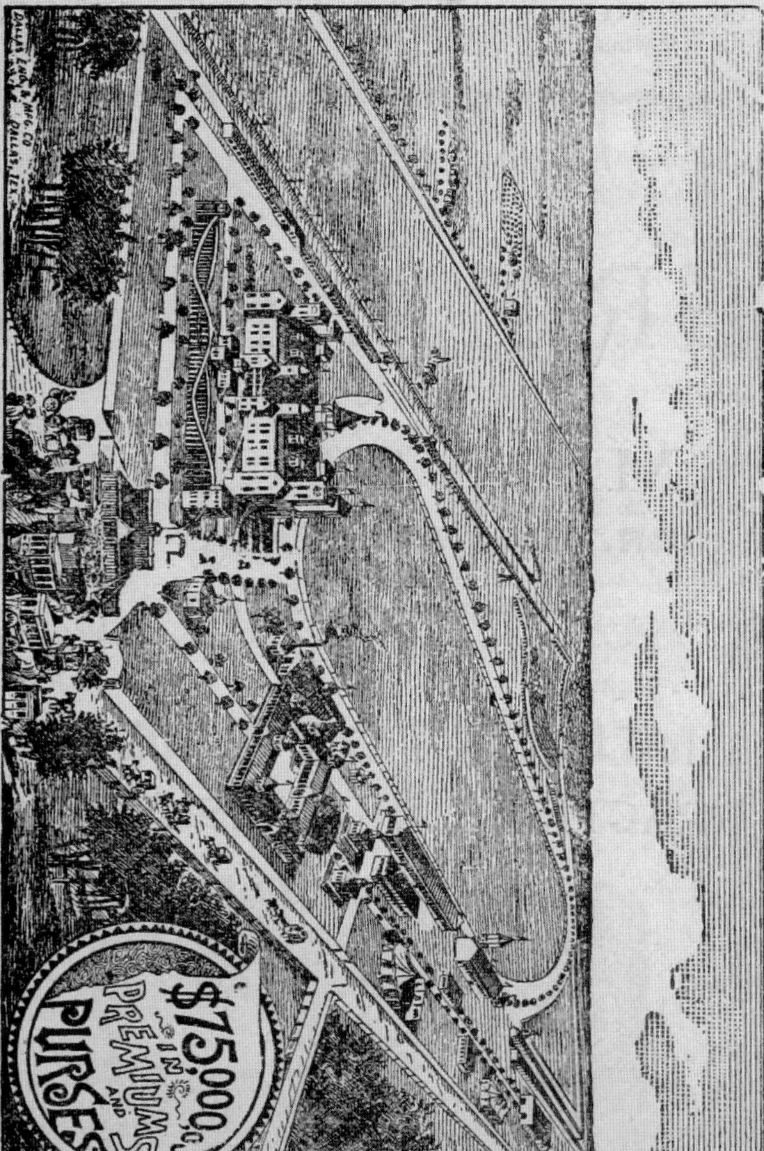

VIEW OF STATE FAIR GROUNDS

—AND—

Dallas Exposition.

THE STATE FAIR.

THE TEXAS STATE FAIR and Dallas Exposition, next to the St. Louis Fair, stands at the head of all State Fairs in the Union, and is the lasting monument of the energy and enterprise of the citizens of Dallas.

The grounds and buildings are located about two and one-half miles east from the court house. It is reached by three lines of electric street railway, the Main street line of the Consolidated Traction Railway Co., the Dallas Rapid Transit Railway Co. and the Elm street line of the Queen City Railway Co.

The grounds have an area of 120 acres, are beautifully ornamented with shade trees and shrubbery of various kinds, supplied with water from the city, the service extending over the entire grounds. There is also an artesian well which supplies the visitors with the purest of water.

The buildings consist of a three-story Exposition hall, 200 x 300 feet, machinery hall, 90 x 300 feet, power hall, 75 x 300 feet, grand stand, 50 x 200 feet, horticultural hall, 60 x 180 feet, hall for exhibition of farm and mill products, 17 x 200 feet, poultry house 13 x 200 feet, geological hall, 43 x 85 feet; music hall with a seating capacity of 3000, stalls of the most modern kind for 800 horses, one row of booths, 20 x 200, another, 48 x 700 feet, a large stock arena, fronted by a large amphitheatre with large seating capacity, and twenty booths underneath a beautiful club house owned by the Dallas Jockey Club. There are two of the finest race

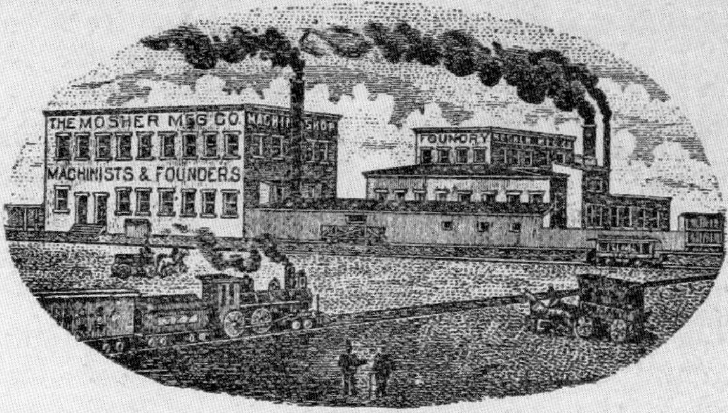

The Mosher Manufacturing Co.

Manufacturers of

House Fronts, Cast Iron and Brass Work. Boxes, Grate Bars, etc. Artesian Well Tools, Electrical Supplies. Architectural Iron Work, Heavy Forging, and Repairs of Engines and Machinery.

Valve Boxes and Water Works Supplies.

OFFICE AND WORKS:
311-317 South Lamar St.
Telephone 377.

Dallas, Texas.

. . . No. 3132 . . .

Capital, $200,000 Surplus, $125,000

The American National Bank.

W. H. THOMAS, Prest.
E. J. GANNON, Cashier.

Dallas, Texas.

tracks in the country, one a mile long and the the other seven-eights of a mile. Although entirely a Dallas enterprise it is an important factor in the development of the state at large.

Do not fail to see the beautiful grounds even though you visit the city when the fair is not in progress. It is a lovely ride and you will feel well repaid for the time.

The Ninth Annual Fair will be held from Oct. 20, to Nov. 4, 1894

Dallas as A Manufacturing Center

—AND—

WHAT SHE HAS

AN idea may be formed of the importance of the industries of Dallas, when it is stated that there are in active and successfull operation, 183 manufactories, with an invested capital of $4,000,000, giving employment to over 4000 laborers, with a yearly pay roll of $2,-$2,000,000. The annual consumption of raw material is valued at $4,000,000, and the output at nearly $7,000,000.

We will endeavor to give a list of the manufactories and some of the enterprising industries of Dallas.

- 1 Architectural Iron Wks.
- 1 Awning Bracket Mfg.
- 2 Badge & Baggage Check.
- 2 Bank & Office Fxtr. Mfrs.
- 1 Billiard Table Mfg.
- 1 Bluing Mfg.
- 5 Boiler Mfg.
- 2 Paper & Wood Box Mfrs.
- 5 Brick Mfrs.
- 5 Broom Mfrs.
- 5 Carriage & Wagon Mfrs.
- 1 Cider Extract Mfr.
- 5 Cigar Factories
- 7 Cornice works
- 1 Corrugated Iron Cistern
- 1 Cotton Machine Mfr.
- 1 Disinfectant Mfr.
- 1 Drain & Sewer Pipe Mfr,
- 6 Foundries
- 1 Hat Mfr.
- 2 Horse Collar Mfrs.
- 2 Ice Mfrs., costing $350,000 (capacity 150 tons each.)
- 1 Artificial Limb Mfg.
- 2 Axle Grease Mfrs.
- 2 Baking Powder Mfrs.
- 3 Bed spring Mfrs.
- 4 Blank Book Mfrs.
- 1 Bluing Mfg.
- 5 Repair shops of Boilers.
- 1 Brewery.
- 1 Pressed Brick Mfr.
- 5 Candy Mfrs.
- 1 Chimney Flue Mfr.
- 1 Cider Mfr.
- 2 Cooperage Works
- 1 Corrugated Iron Roofing
- 4 Cotton Gin Mfrs.
- 1 Creamery
- 3 Door, Window & Screen
- 2 Flouring Mills
- 1 Gas Works
- 1 Horn Furniture Mfr.
- 1 Ink Roller Factory
- 2 Iron Fencing & Roofing
- 2 Jelly, & Preserves Mfrs.

2 Jewelry Mfrs.
2 Line Mfrs.
7 Matress Mfrs.
1 Overall and Pants Mfr.
1 Packing House
3 Planing Mills
2 Rubber Stamp Mfrs.
3 Shirt Factories
1 Show Case Mfr.
4 Soda & Sarsaparilla Wks.
4 Ginger Ale & Bot. Works
1 Tannery
2 Tent, Awning and Wagon Cover Mfrs.
3 Vinegar Works
2 Yeast "
*1 Cotton Mill
5 Steam Laundries
3 Marble Works
7 Medicine Mfrs.
2 Paint Mfrs.
1 Paper Mill
1 Printer's Roller Factory
8 Saddlery and Harness
2 Shoe Findings
3 Soap Mfrs.
2 Stone Saw Mills
2 Tank Builders
1 Trunk Factory.
9 Tin, Copper and Sheet Iron works
1 Well Curbing Mfr.
1 Whiffltree. "

*The cotton mill having 13,000 spindles and 300 looms. This mill employs 200 hands. The Company operate a capital of $4,000,000.

The products of these factories here generally find their way into all towns of Texas and many of them are shipped to Arkansas, Louisiana, Indian Territory, Arizona, New Mexico, Colorado, Utah and Washington.

Dallas ranks first in population in the state.

Dallas has a population of 62,000.

Dallas is the wholesale center of the Southwest.

Dallas is the most cosmopolitan city.

Dallas has water works costing $1,500,000.

Dallas has the largest auditorium in the South, ctpable of seating 10,000 people.

Dallas has 50 churches valued at $200,000.

Dallas school property is valued at $2,000,000.

Dallas has three fine colleges valued at $1,000,000.

Dallas has two of the best business colleges in the Southwest.

Dallas has the only telegraph college in the state.

Dallas has 50 miles of street railway.

Dallas has five banks with a combined capital of $4,000,000.

Dallas has the largest and most systematically arranged post-office in the Southwest.

Dallas has the largest and most beautiful court house in Texas, valued at $500,000.

Dallas has two of the largest ice factories in the state.

Dallas hotels are unexcelled in the whole South.

Dallas has ten railroads reaching out in every direction.

Dallas has unsurpassed shipping facilities.

Dallas is the second largest implement and machine market in the world.

Dallas is surrounded by the most fertile land in the world.

Dallas has 183 manufactories.

Dallas is the center of the greatest cotton, wheat and corn producing territory in the state.

One-third the cotton grown in the state, is within a radius of 100 miles of Dallas; also one-third the wheat and one-half the corn.

Dallas is at the head of navigation—a stream reaching to the gulf of Mexico—part of the same is open for navigation.

Chicago & Alton R.R.

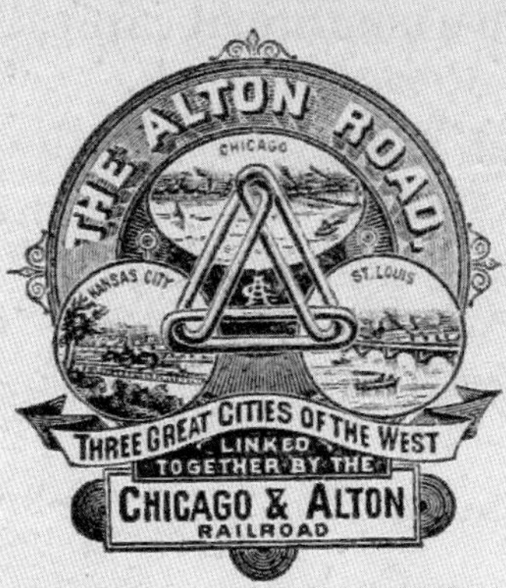

Perfect Passenger Service

Solid Vestibuled Trains

ASK THE TICKET AGENT ABOUT

The Chicago Limited

FROM

St. Louis

TO

Chicago.

A Pullman Vestibuled Train. Leaves St. Louis 8:45 a. m., arrives Chicago 4:55 p. m. same day. Runs Daily over the

Chicago & Alton R. R.

W. H. ABEL, Southwestern Passenger Agent,
Grand Windsor Building,
P. O. Box W. DALLAS, TEXAS.

In view of these facts, we ask you to seriously consider the advisability of making an investment. In a few years at the fartherest, it will bring you a handsome competency, that will earn you a reputation among your friends as being a far-seeing and wise investor.

Now is the time.

SUMMARY.

If you are seeking a comfortable home in a progressive city, a location for a manufacturing plant. a place for a jobbing house of any description, a desirable location to go into the live stock business, or if you desire to make a profitable investment in real estate, it will pay you to investigate the advantages of Dallas.

If you are a merchant in a territory tributary to Dallas, it will pay you to buy in Dallas.

If you are a live stock shipper it will pay you to ship to Dallas.

If you are a grain dealer in Dallas territory, it will pay you to ship to Dallas.

If you are a banker it will pay you to keep an account with a Dallas bank.

If you wish to buy grain, live stock, packing house products, or anything manufactured or sold in Dallas. it will pay you to write to Dallas for prices.

If you are a merchant, live stock dealer, grain dealer, in any territory tributary to Dallas, and have any trouble in the way of freight rates, time of trains, delayed shipments, or any other question of transportation that prevents your using Dallas markets, if you will report same to the Dallas Commercial Club, it will be investigated and remedied if the situation justifies the railroads in doing so.

DALLAS COTTON MILLS

W. C. HOWARD, Prest.
A. F. HARDIE,
Sec. & Treas.

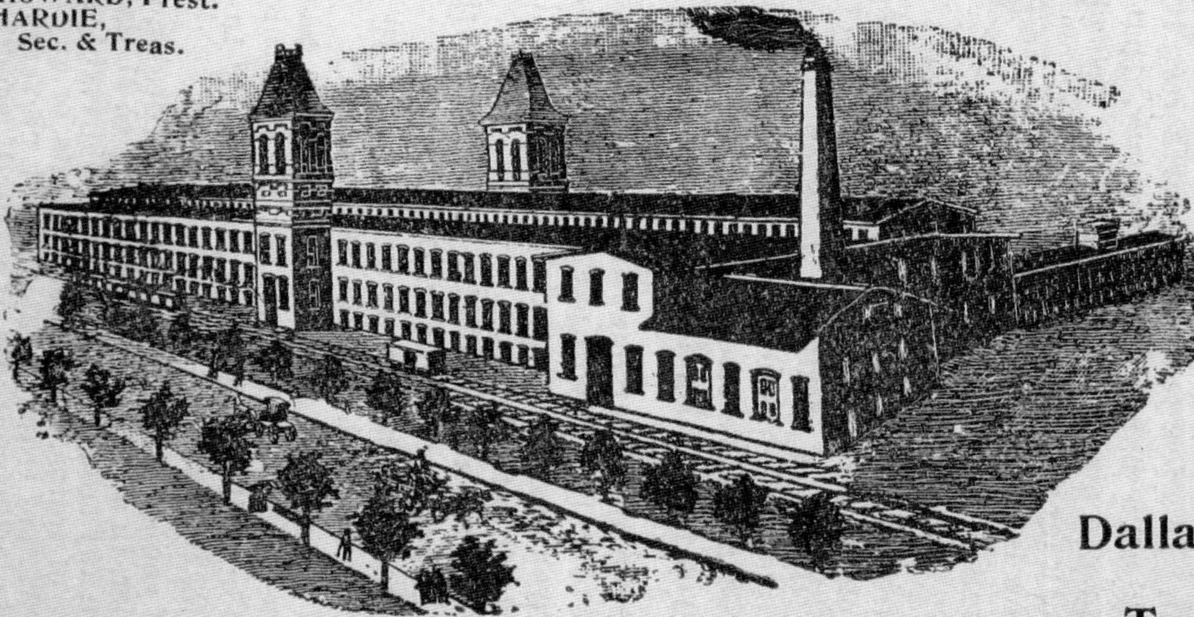

Dallas,

Texas.

Manufacturers of DUCKS, OSNABURGS, SHEETINGS, DRILLS & KNITTING COTTONS
DENIMS, TICKS and CHEVIOTS. Capacity, 200,000 yards per Week.

WHAT DALLAS WANTS.

"Seek and ye Shall Find."

IN THESE days of newspapers, telegraph, telephone, railroad and commercial agencies; as well as the thousand other sources of reliable information, it is an easy matter for an investor, when he cannot look over the ground in person to inform himself as to where his money will be wisely invested.

No city in the world can equal Dallas as a field for factories, as well as all other classes of industry.

The raw material for nearly all kinds of such industries is within easy reach, and there is no place where capital will be so sure to reap an abundant and speedy reward as in the manufacturing business here.

Upon investigation we find that any of the following manufactories and industries would receive the hearty co-operation of the citizens of Dallas.

Paper Mills
Starch Factories
Boiler Works
Glass "
Salt "
Iron and Steel Works
Knitting Factories
Cotton & Woolen Factories
Shoe and Rubber "
Clothing "
Piano and Organ "
Castor Oil "
Stove Works
Nail "
Agricultural Implements
Overall Factories
Breweries
Ax and Broom Handles
Canning Factories
Pickling "
Sugar Beet Industries
Roller Mills
Foundries
Bagging Factories
Chair "
Furniture "
Watch "
Basket "
Potteries
Type Foundries
Charcoal Industries
Packing Houses
Carriages and Wagons
Saur Kraut works
Round Houses and Repair Shops

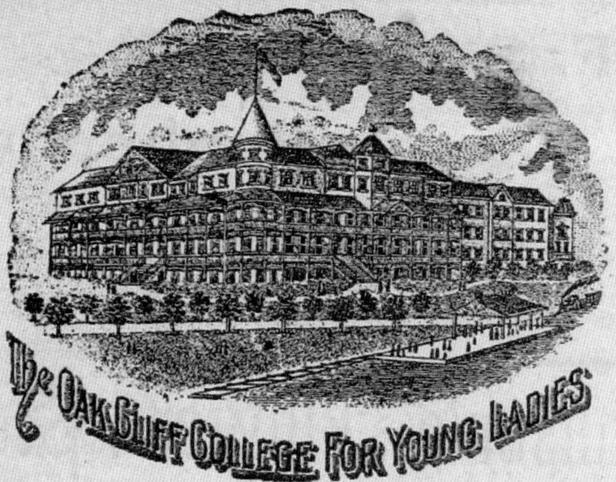

EDUCATIONAL FACILITIES.

THERE is no part of Dallas enterprise to which her citizens point with more pride than her educational system. The period of study extends through a course of twelve years and the schools are open to pupils ranging from the ages of seven to twenty-one.

The departments are primary, intermediate and high school.

The city school property is valued at $347,000.

EXPENSES.

Table of expense for maintaining the Public Free Schools of the City of Dallas, for the past scholastic year.

Superintendent's Salary	$2,000.00
Teachers' pay roll	58,019.70
Janitors' " "	4.434.00
Secretary's salary	875.00
Expense and supplies	1801.35
Repairs	2463.80
Fuel	2621.55
Insurance	1526.79
Total	$73,741.19

STATISTICAL TABLE

SCHOOLS.	Total Enrollment.	Per cent. of Attendance.
High School	649	94.2
East Dallas	519	96
Cumberland Hill	475	95.5
McKinney Avenue	425	97.3
Cedar Lawn	399	96.5
Oak Grove	457	95
San Jacinto	370	96 5
Columbian School	377	95
Alamo School	196	95
Total. White	3867	95.9
COLORED SCHOOLS.		
High School	565	96
School No. 1	298	95.7
School No. 2	276	97.5
School No. 3	137	97 3
Total, Colored	1270	96.4
Grand Total, White and Colored	5137	96
For the year	5137	95.2
For last year	5030	95.2

Besides the public schools there are the Oak Cliff College, Ursuline Academy, St. Mary's Orphanage and St. Mary's Institute (Episcopal), are well equipped schools and have won a fair share of patronage.

The curriculm of these institutions of learning compare favorably with much older and better endowed schools of their kind in the older states. It will be observed that Dallas is a city in which the best possible educational advantages in the Southwest can be secured at a very small expense.

SPECIALTIES:

- Snow Flake Oil
- Sunbeam Oil
- White Rose Gasoline
- Cold Test Cylinder Oil
- Black Diamond Cylinder Oil
- Crown Engine Oil

The Eagle Refining Co.

Headquarters for HIGH GRADE **OILS**

A. W. CLEM, Mgr.

Telephone 465 *DALLAS, TEXAS.*

RENTAL BUSINESS SOLICITED.

METROPOLITAN LAND BUREAU

L. A. WILSON, MANAGER.

281 Main Street, . . . Dallas, Texas.

FOR SALE OR TRADE, ALL KINDS OF

REAL ESTATE, CATTLE, HORSES,
MERCHANDISE,
BUSINESS CHANCES Etc.

Fleischman & Co.

Manufacturers of

COMPRESSED
. . . YEAST . . .

BOX 314. DALLAS, TEXAS.

The state endowment of the common schools is very large, and is worthy the attention of the whole world. In the neighborhood of $7,427,808.75 in interest bearing bonds; more than $14,380.906.37 in interest bearing bond notes, and about 20,000,000 acres of unsold lands constitute the state endowment. In addition to this, the state has granted to each county four leagues of land, which constitute the county endowment.

Texas will soon be dotted over and over with magnificent school buildings and colleges. It is almost so now, but in ten years it will lead every other state in the Union.

DALLAS CHURCH DIRECTORY.

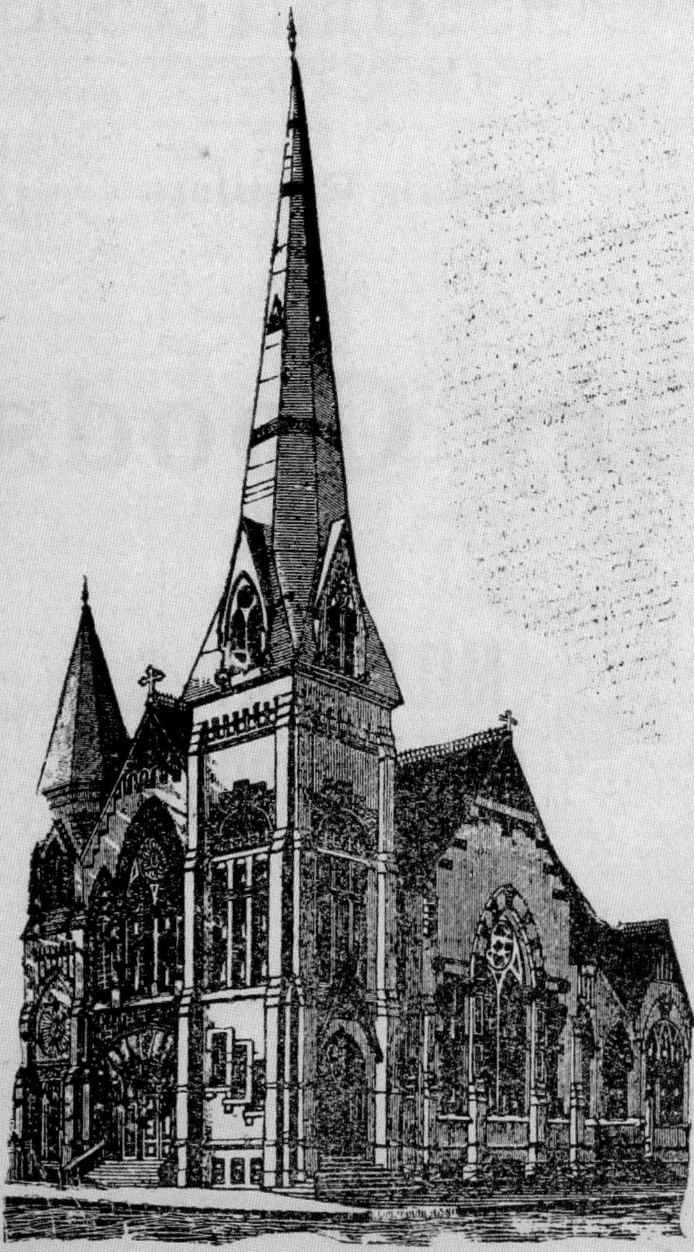

FIRST BAPTIST CHURCH.

EPISCOPAL.

St. Matthews' Cathedral, Episcopal, South Ervay St., corner of Canton. Rt. Rev. A. C. Garrett. D D. L L. D. Bishop. Services on Sunday, 11 a. m. and 8 p. m. Holy communion every Sunday at 7:30 a. m., and also at the 11 a. m. service on the first Sunday in the month. Sunday school at 9:30 a. m.

Church of Incarnation, corner McKinney and Harwood. Rev. E. Wickens, pastor; Col. Oliver Steele, Supt. Sunday school. The Church Club for the men, meets every Monday at 8 p. m.; Mr. J. Catto, president. The Ladies' Aid Society meets every Monday at 4 p. m. Mrs. W. M. Edwards, president, Mrs. B. Fallon, treasurer. The Altar Guide meets as occasion requires; Mrs. M. Chambers, president.

CATHOLIC.

Sacred Heart Pro-Cathedral, corner Bryan and N. Ervay streets, Rt. Rev. E. J. Dunne, bishop; services on Sunday, low mass at 8 o'clock, high mass and sermon at 10:30 a. m., catechism at 3 p. m., vespers and sermon at 7:30 p. m.

St. Patrick's Church, corner of S. Harwood and Eakin streets; services on Sunday, low mass at 7:30 a. m., high mass and sermon at 10:30 a. m., catechism at 3 p. m., mass during the week at 8 a. m.

BAPTIST.

First Baptist Church, corner of Ervay street and Patterson avenue, Rev. C. L Seasholes, pastor. Sunday school at 9:30 a. m., W. R. Howell, superintendent; preaching at 11 a. m. and 7:30 p. m. prayer meeting every Wednesday at 7:30 p. m.; young folks meeting at 6:30 p. m.

Second Baptist Church, South Ervay street. Preaching at 11 a. m. and 7:30 p. m.; Sunday school, 9:30 a. m., T. M. Macdonnell, pastor.

First Baptist Church, of Oak Cliff, Rev. A. M. Croxton, pastor. Preaching at 11 a. m., Sunday school at 9:30 a. m., L. M. Farrish, superintendent; prayer meeting at 7 o'clock, p. m. Wednesday.

Washington Avenue Baptist Church, Oak Cliff; services at 11 a. m. and 8:15 p. m, Austin H. Mitchell, pastor; Sunday school, 11 a. m., Young People's meeting at 8 p. m.

Lake Ave. Mission Church, preaching 7:30 p. m., Sunday school at 9:30 a. m., Prof. Coleman, superintendent. Young Folks' meeting every Tuesday night at 7:45.

Crowdus Street Mission. Sunday school, 3 p. m., preaching 4 p. m., first and fourth Sundays in each month.

Allen Street Mission. Preaching at 11 a. m., Sunday school at 3 p. m.

METHODIST.

First Methodist Episcopal Church, South, Commerce street, near the post-office; services 11 a. m. and 8 p. m. Rev. E. L. Spraggins, pastor. Young People's meeting in the basement at 6:45 p m., B. M. Burgher, superintendent; general prayer meeting Wednesday at 7.30 o'clock p. m.

City Mission; L. A. Hanson, pastor. Preaching at East Dallas, corner Haskell and Attison streets, every Sunday at 11 a. m. and 7:30 p. m.; Sunday school at 9:30 a. m., E. W. Ingle, superintendent; prayer meeting Wednesday at 7:20 p. m.

St Mark's M. E. Church, South, Oak Cliff. Rev. N. B. Read, pastor; preaching, 11 a. m. and 7:30 p. m.; Sabbath School at 9:30 a. m., M. W. Crow, superintendent. General prayer meeting, Wednesday night.

South Oak Cliff M. E. Church, South, Mission. Sabbath school, 3 p. m., Judge Thomas, superintendent.

Tabernacle M. E. Church, corner of St. Paul and Main streets, Rev. A. P. Morrison, D. D., pastor. Morning service, 11 a. m., evening service, 7:30 p. m; Sunday school, 10 a. m., Wm. McKee, superintendent. Epworth League meets at 6:30 p. m. Prayer meeting every Wednesday at 7:30 p. m. Masonic Avenue M. E. mission school meets every Sunday at 3 p. m., Chas. R. Jones, superintendent.

Hope Mission, 173 Cochran street, near Griffin, A. P. Morrison, D. D., pastor. Sunday school, 3 p. m., for children and adults; preaching every Sunday at 4 p. m. Lessons in singing free, Tuesday; prayer meeting, Thursday, 7:30.

PAUL GIRAUD,

. . . Draughtsman

313 MAIN STREET.

Drawing and Lithograph Engraving of Cities, Bird's Eye Views, a Specialty.

Apply or Write to PAUL GIRAUD, Dallas, Texas.

A. WATSON,

CONTRACTOR AND BUILDER.

ESTIMATES GIVEN ON ALL KINDS OF BUILDINGS.

P. O. BOX 341.

RESIDENCE, 135 Sanger Aveuue,

DALLAS, - - TEXAS.

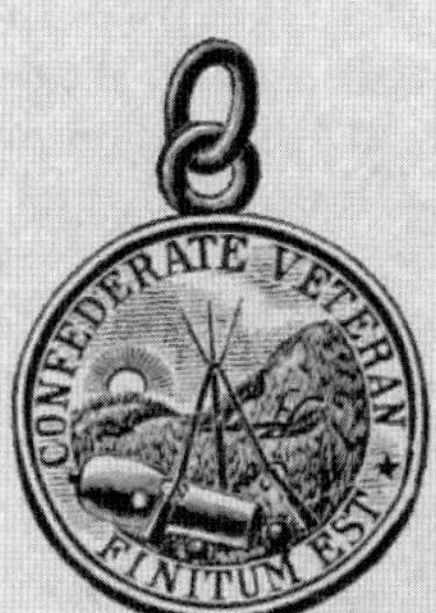

CONFEDERATE EMBLEMS,

Lapel and Sleeve Buttons, Charms, Pins, Souvenir Spoons & Walking Canes.

FRANK EDWARDS,

North Texas Bank Bldg.,

DALLAS, TEXAS.

Floyd Street M. E. Church, South, Rev. W. F. Clark, pastor. Preaching every Sunday at 11 a. m. and 7:15 p. m.; Sunday school at 9:30 a. m, S. H. McBride, superintendent. Prayer meeting Wednesday at 7:30 p. m.

West Dallas St. Paul, Rev. B. A. Tommasson, pastor. Preaching first Sunday at 8 a. m. and 7:30 p. m., and on the third Sunday at 3:30 p. m., and at Rush Chapel every third Sunday at 11 a. m.

Trinity M. E. Church, South, corner of Trinidad and Phelps streets, North Dallas, P. L. Smith, pastor. Preaching at 11 a. m. and 7:15 p. m. Sabbath school at 9:30 a. m.. Wm. Rogers, superintendent. General prayer meeting Thursday night at 7:15 o'clock. Epworth League meets every Sunday at 6:30 p. m.

South Dallas M. E. Church, South, at City Park Presbyterian Church, corner Gano and Snodgrass Sts., J. F. Archer, pastor. Preaching at 11 a. m. and 7:45 p. m.: Sunday school, T. B. Corpening, superintendent, meets from 3 to 4 p. m. Epworth League (young people's meeting) at 6:45 p. m. Epworth League Mission Sunday school, C. L. Dealey, superintendent, meets on Corinth, between Wall street and Cockrell avenue, each Sunday at 4:15 p. m.

Oak Lawn, E. C. McVoy, pastor; services every Sunday at 11 a m. and 7:30 p. m. Sunday school at 9:30 a. m. J. D. Cullom, superintendent. Prayer meeting Wednesday at 7:30.

PRESBYTERIAN.

First Presbyterian Church, corner of Main and Harwood streets, Rev. A. P. Smith, D. D., pastor; services at 11 a. m. and 7:30 p. m. Sabbath school at 9:30 a. m., Capt. J. M. McCoy and Mr. R. S. Price, superintendents. Prayer meeting Wednesday at 8 p. m.

Second Presbyterian Church, northeast corner Harwood and Wood streets, Rev. Warner B. Riggs, pastor; services 11 a. m. and 7:30 p m. Sunday school 9:30 a. m. Prayer meeting Wednesday, 7:45 p. m. Children's meeting, Wednesday, 4 p. m. All are invited.

Oak Cliff: Preaching at 11 a. m.

Cumberland Presbyterian Church, (in Seymour Bldg.) College Station, Oak Cliff, Rev. G. W. Templeton, pastor; J. H. Gillispie, superintendent Sunday school. Preaching every Sunday at 11 a. m. and 8 p. m. Sunday school at 9:30 a. m.

First Cumberland Presbyterian Church, Harwood, between Live Oak and Bryan. John D. Hunter, pastor. Preaching every Sunday at 11 a. m. and 8 p. m. Sunday school at 9:45 a. m., R. B. Seay, superintendent.

Exposition Park Presbyterian Church, Parry avenue, foot of Third avenue, Rev. Dr. May, pastor; Sunday school, 9:45 a. m, Mrs G. W. North, superintendent. Preaching 11 a. m.; prayer meeting Thursday evening.

Westminster Presbyterian Church, corner of McKinney and Thomas avenues and Phelps street. Rev. Jas. D. McLean, pastor. Preaching at 11 a. m. and 7:45 p. m. Sabbath school at 9:45 a. m.; Y. P. S. C. E. prayer meeting at 6:10 p. m., general prayer meeting Friday at 7:30 p. m.

City Park Presbyterian Church, near the corner of South Browder and Gano streets. Sunday school at 9:30 a. m, L. A. Wilson, superintendent; preaching at 11 a. m. and 8 p. m., by Rev. S. D. McLean, pastor. Prayer meeting and service of song every Wednesday evening at 8 o'clock.

Bethany Presbyterian Church, corner Highland and Ashland streets, Rev. S. W. Patterson, pastor. Preaching at 11 a. m. m. and 7 p m. Sunday school 3 p. m., J. E. Muncey, superintendent. Prayer meeting, Wednesday, 7:30; Teacher's meeting, Thursday 8 p. m.

CONGREGATIONAL.

Corner of Harwood and Bryan streets, Rev. C. I. Scofield, pastor; services 11 a. m. and 8 p m. Sunday school 9:30 a. m., Mrs. C. T. Dickinson, superintendent. Society Christian Endeavor, 7 p. m. Prayer meeting. Wednesday at 8 p. m.

Grand Avenue Branch of Congregational Church, Rev. C. I. Scofield, pastor; Rev. W. I Carroll, assistant pastor. Preaching every Sunday at 11 a. m. and 8 p. m. Sunday school at 3 p. m., T. J. Jones, superintendent. Prayer meeting Thursday at 8 p. m.

Congregational Gospel Mission, Elm street, opposite North street. Sunday school at 3 p. m.; gospel services 8 p. m. every Sunday. Bible reading 8 p. m. every Thursday.

CHRISTIAN.

Central Christian Church, corner Masten and Patterson avenues, Rev. M. M. Davis, pastor. Preaching 11 a. m. and 8 p. m. Sunday school 9:30 a. m., S. Y. Trice, superintendent. Chinese Sunday school, 12:30 p. m., S. Y. Trice, superintendent. Y. P. S. C. E., senior and junior, 6:30 p. m., Mrs. E. Hamilton, superintendent of junior; A. A. Everitts, president, senior; Miss Arsalie Coffin, vice-president. Business meeting every first Tuesday in each month. Prayer meeting every Wednesday at 7:45 p. m.; choir practice, Friday at 8 p. m. Ladies' Aid Society meets every Tuesday at 2:30 p. m.

HEBREW.

The Ladies' Hebrew Benevolent Association, Mrs. S Heidenigsfelder, president; Mrs. L. Goslin, vice-president; Mrs. E. M. Chapman, treasurer; Mrs. L. A. Cahn, financial secretary; Simon Loeb, recording secretary. Meets first Wednesday in each month.

Little Helping Society composed of children from nine to fourteen years of age. Bessie Chapman, president; Hattie Tillman, vice-president; Julia Chapman, secretary; Mabelle Cohene, treasurer. Hon. officers: Mrs. D. G. Oppenheim, president; Mrs. E. M. Chapman, vice-president; Mrs. S. Heidenigsfelder, secretary and Mrs. J. Cahn, treasurer. Meets every Wednesday afternoon.

Gentlemen's Hebrew Benevolent Association. Alex. Ortleb, president; Dr. E. M. Chapman, vice-president; M. Goettienger, secretary and treasurer. Meets in January of each year.

SALVATION ARMY.

Dallas Corps No. 548, 288 Commerce street.

SPIRITUALIST.

First Spiritual Society, corner Ervay and Marilla Sts.

COLORED CHURCHES.

Bethel A. M. E., corner Cochran and Leonard Sts.
Evening Chapel M. E., 289 Juliet St.
Free Mission Baptist, 115 Boll St.
Free Will Baptist, corner Hall and Cochran Sts.
Macedonia Baptist, 116 Montezuma St
Mt. Rose Baptist, corner William & Henry Sts.
Mt. Zion Baptist, 268 South Lamar St.
New Hope Baptist, corner San Jacinto and Bogel Sts.
New Zion Baptist, corner Alamo and Ervin Sts.
Plymouth Congregational Church, 296 N. Hawkins St.
Salem Baptist Church, 401 South Preston St.
St. James A. M. E. Church, 421 Young St.
St. Paul's M. E. Church, corner Juliet and Burford Sts.
Trinity Baptist Church, 429 William St.
Young St. Christian Church, corner Young & Marilla.

Young Men's Christian Association.

OFFICERS.

J. P. Jackson, Gen'l Sec. B. P. Fakes, President.
C. H. Edwards. Vice-Pres. R. Myrick, Treasurer.
F. N. Foot. Recording Secretary.
F. B. Sinex. Membership and Financial Secretary.
Chas. H. Carey, Physical Director.

DIRECTORS.

B. P. Fakes. B. M. Burgher,
C. H. Edwards, L. R. Wright,
H. N. Goodwin, Jno. W. Springer,
M. P. Moody, R. B. Harwood,
S. Y. Trice, W. K. Homan,
R. Myrick, A. F. Hardie.
F. N. Foot. W. S. Simkins, R C. Ayers.

The emblem of the Association is the red triangle, representing sides of the man—Spirit, Mind and Body.

The following figures will give some idea of the history and growth of the work.

Organized Nov. 5, 1885.

	1888.	189?.	1893.	1894.
Total Membership...........	130	253	403	548
Average Daily Attendance.	31	115	126	201
Av. Attnd'c. Sun. Meeting.	18	54	33	106
Value Furniture and Aprts.	$400	$——	$2000	$3500

Star Course of Entertainments for 1894-'95:

Nov. 8—Schubert Male Quartette of Chicago.
" 20—Thos. Dixon, Jr. of New York.
Dec. 11—A. D. French, of Chicago (Chalk Talk).
" 18—Dr. A. A. Willetts of Dayton, Ohio.
Jan. ..—Sweedish Quartette Concert Co. of Boston.
Feb. 7—Prof. J. B. De Motte of Indiana.
" 19—Ovide Musin Concert Co.
Mch. 28—Robarts Harper (Monte Carlo).

The many privileges of the Association include the following.

Parlors and Amusement Rooms, Reading Room and Library, Lectures and Entertainments, Gymnasium and Bath Rooms, Gospel meetings and Bible classes.

Membership Fee $5.00 per year.

Any young man of good moral character is eligible to membership.

Strangers welcome.

C. S. Hartman,

Contractor AND Builder

Brick and Stone Building a Specialty.

THOROUGH AND PERFECT WORK
. . . AND . . .
SATISFACTION GUARANTEED.

C. S. HARTMAN,
Corner Armstrong and Kentucky Streets,
DALLAS, - - TEXAS.

Vendig Bros. Shirt Co.

Shirts, Underwear,
Night Robes, Etc.

Special Attention Given to Orders by Mail.
We Retain Records of All Measurements.

224 Elm Street, Dallas, Texas.

Union Fish and Oyster Depot

WM. HUNT, Proprietor.
——DEALER IN——
. . . Vegetables and Fish . . .
FRUITS, CANDIES AND CIGARS.

580 Elm St., Dallas, Texas.

SECRET SOCIETIES.

MASONIC.

Masonic Hall, corner Main and Murphy streets.

Dallas Chapter No. 1, O. E. S , meet last Thursday of each month.

Dallas Chapter No. 47, R. A. M., meet first Monday of each month.

Dallas Com'ndry, No. 6, K. T., meet first Thursday of each month.

Hella Temple A. A. O. N. of M. S., meet third Thursday of each month.

Tannehill Lodge No. 52, A. F. & A. M., meet second and last Tuesday of each month.

ODD FELLOWS.

Odd Fellows' Hall, corner Main and Austin Sts.

Dallas Lodge No. 44, meet every Wednesday night.

Ridgley Encampment, No. 25, meet first and third Friday each month.

Trinity Lodge, No. 198, meet every Tuesday night.

KNIGHTS OF PYTHIAS.

Amity Lodge No. 108, meet every Tuesday night, 345 Main street.

Columbian Lodge No. 160, meet every Friday night, 345 Main street.

Cœur de Lion Division No. 5, U. R., meet 3rd Saturday each month, 345 Main street.

Cœur de Lion, Lodge, No. 8, meet every Thursday night, 345 Main street.

Dallas Division, No. 18 U. R., meet third Friday night, 381 Elm street.

Dallas Lodge, No. 70, meet every Monday night, 381 Elm street.

Endowment Rank Sec. 177, meet last Friday each month, 345 Main street.

Endowment Rank, Sec. 830, meet last Friday each month, 381 Elm street.

KNIGHTS OF HONOR.

Dallas Lodge No. 1570, meet first and third Thursday night, 381 Elm street.

Dallas Commandry No. 27 U. R., meets every Monday night at Turner Hall.

Queen City Lodge No. 941, meet 2d and 4th Tuesday, I. O. O. F. Hall.

Teutonia Lodge No. 1873, meet 2d and 4th Thursday, 81 Elm street.

Dallas Lodge No 1593, K. & L. of H., meet 1st and 3rd Thursday, Temperance Hall.

GRAND ARMY OF THE REPUBLIC.

Geo. H. Thomas Post No. 6, meet 2d and 4th Wednesday, 381 Elm street.

John A. Dix Post No. 11, meet 1st and 3rd Wednesday, 381 Elm street.

HEBREW.

Ahavath Sholom Lodge, No. 346, I. O. B. B., meet 1st and 3rd Tuesday, 292 Commerce street.

Dallas Lodge, No. 199, I. O. B. B., meets 2d and 4th Tuesday, 292 Commerce street.

Jacob Frees Lodge, No. 1, O. B. A., meet 3rd Sunday each month, 381 Elm street.

Lone Star Lodge, No. 197, I. O. F. S. of I., meet 1st and 3rd Monday 292 Commerce street.

Lone Star Lodge, No. 162, O. K. S. B., meet 2d and 4th Monday, 292 Commerce street.

CATHOLIC KNIGHTS OF AMERICA.

St. Joseph Branch No. 678, meet 1st and 3rd Sunday, corner Harwood and Eakin streets.

St. Patrick's Branch No. 70, meet 1st and 3rd Sunday, Bryan and Cottage Lane.

TEMPERANCE.

Dallas Lodge No. 2, I. O. G. T., meet every Tuesday, 349 Main street.

South Dallas Lodge No. 10, I. O. G. T., meet Monday South Dallas M. E. Church.

MISCELLANEOUS SOCIETIES.

Branch 132 Nat'l Association of Letter Carriers, meet 1st Tuesday each month, post-office.

Columbia Lodge, No. 65, O. of S. of H., meet 1st and 3rd Sunday, Odd Fellows' Hall.

Columbian Lodge No. 158, A. O. U. W., meets 2d and 4th Wednesday, 349 Main street.

Dallas Amateur Athletic Club, meet at Hall, 416-418 Jackson street.

Dallas Lodge, No. 25, Ry. Emp. F. B. Association meet 1st and 3rd Tuesday, 289 Main St.

Dallas Wheel Club, meet 1st Wednesday, 416 Jackson street.

Fraternal Mystic Circle, meets 2d and 4th Eriday, Odd Fellows Hall.

Liquor Dealer's Assn., meet 2d and 4th Friday, 381 Elm street.

Post E. Texas Division, T. P. A., meet Sunday morning, Trust Co. Bldg.

Dallas Lodge, No. 106, A. O. U. W., meet

J. SUNDERLAND,
445 Thomas Avenue.

W. G. WHITLOCK,
179 Texas Street.

Whitlock & Sunderland,

Carpenters and Builders,

GENERAL REPAIR SHOP.

472 Main Street, DALLAS, TEXAS,

Cor. Main and Harwood Sts.

BUY A

Davis Automatic Ink Stand

The Ink exposed only at each dipping of the pen. Prevents all evaporation. Never thickens. It will soon save its cost in ink. Send two cent stamp for Illustrated Catalogue.

THOS. J. ROBBERSON, State Agent,
314 West Jones Street, SHERMAN, TEXAS.

Only member of the American Ticket Brokers' Association in Dallas.

KAISER'S Railway Ticket Office

Reduced Rates to all Points.

Sleeping Car Berths Secured.

236 MAIN STREET,
DALLAS, TEXAS.

C. H. STUART,

... THE ORIENTAL TAILOR

SUITS to Order, $15.00 up. PANTS from $5.00 up.

Cleaning, Dyeing and Repairing Neatly Done.

114 AKARD STREET,

DALLAS, - - TEXAS.

Dallas Lodge No. 71, B. P. O. E., meet every Tuesday night, 285 Main street.

Comet Council No. 5, O. C. F., meet 2d and 4th Thursday, 292 Commerce street.

Dallas Frohsinn, meet every Wednesday night, Turner Hall.

Dallas Gruteli Verein, meet 2d and 4th Saturday, corner Preston and Cabell streets.

Dallas Turn Verein, meet 1st and 3rd Monday, Turner Hall.

Fidelity Lodge No. 410, A. L. of H., meet 2d and 4th Tuesday.

Texas Camp No. 1, Woodmen of the World, meet 1st and 3rd Tuesday night, 381 Elm street.

Texas Lodge No. 33, O. of G. C., meet 2d and 4th Friday, corner Preston and Cabell streets.

Uhland Lodge No. 22, O. of S. H., meet 2d and 4th Sunday, Odd Fellows Hall.

Young Men's Christian Association, rooms Elm street.

Societa Roma of Dallas, meet 1st and 3rd Monday, Schaub's Hall

Son's of Veterans U. S. A., meet 2d and 4th Wednesday, 349 Main street.

Spanish American Society, meet Tuesdays and Saturdays Commercial Bus. College.

Sterling Price Camp C. V. No. 31, U. C. V., meet 2d Tuesday, 289 Main street.

Irish American Benevolent Association, meets 1st and 3rd Wednesdays.

Trans-Mississippi Dept. U. C. F., headquarters 280 Main street.

LABOR ORGANIZATIONS.

Assn. Union 29, of T. & S. C. Workers, meet every Friday, Schaub's hall.

Bakers' Union No. 90, meet 1st and 3rd Saturday, Schaub's hall.

Bricklayers' Protective Union No. 5, meet every Monday, Schaub's hall.

B. L. I. P. U. No. 1, of Texas, meet every Saturday, Schaub's hall.

Cigar Makers' Local Union No 262, meet 1st and 3rd Tuesday, Schaub's hall.

Dallas Branch Am. Federation of Labor, meet 1st and 3rd Sunday, Labor hall.

Dallas Branch Journeymen Stone Cutters, meet 2d and 4th Tuesday, Schaub's hall.

Dallas Lodge, No. 46, B. & D. of A., meeet 1st and 3rd Wednesday, Labor hall.

Dallas Press Feeders' Union No. 10, meet 1st Friday, Labor hall.

Dallas Pressmen's Union No. 46, meet 2d Monday, Labor hall.

Dallas Saddle and Harnessmakers' Union, No. 18, meet 2d and 4th Saturday, Schaub's hall.

Dallas Typographical Union No. 173, meet 1st Sunday, 381 Elm street.

Local Assembly, No. 1931, K. of L., meet every Thursday, Labor hall.

Local Union, No. 198, B. of C. & J. of A., meet every Friday, Labor hall.

Local No. 48, Nat'l League of Musicians, meet 1st and 3rd Sunday, Mayer's Garden.

Operative Plasterers' Union, No. 61, meet every Thursday, Schaub's hall.

Union Band, meet every Sunday, Mayer's Garden.

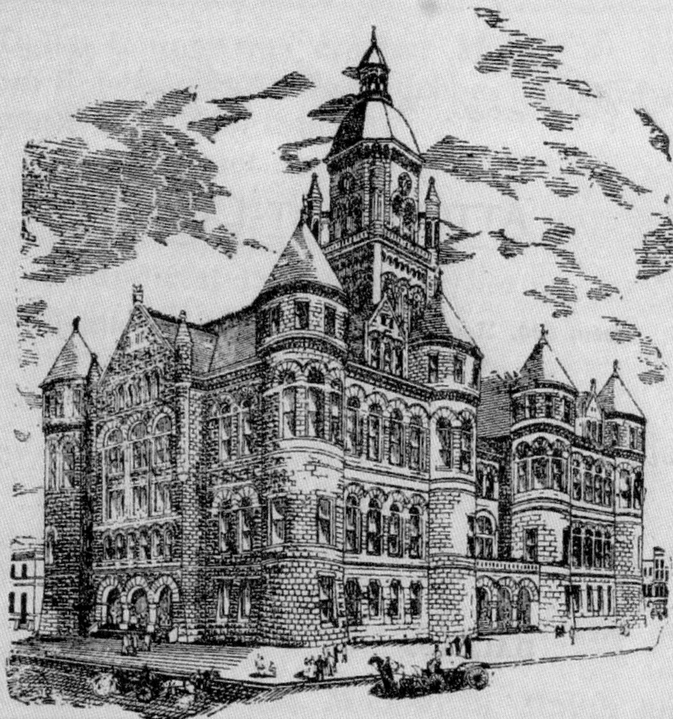

(DALLAS COUNTY COURT HOUSE.)

COUNTY OFFICERS.

Judge.............................T. F. Nash
Clerk...........................L. H. Hughes
Attorney.....................Jno. P. Gillispie
Treasurer...........................W. N. Coe
Surveyor.........................J. M. Young
Assessor...........................J. T. Bolton
Collector.......................Louis Jacoby
Sheriff.............................Ben Cabell

DISTRICT OFFICERS.

County Criminal Dist. Judge....Chas. F. Clint
Fourteenth Dist. Judge.......Robt. E. Burke
Forty-fourth Dist. Judge.........Edward Gray
District Clerk.................Joe H. Stewart

Dallas County was named after G. M. Dallas.
Dallas County has an aera of 900 square miles.

Dallas County was created March 30, 1846, from Robertson and Nacogdoches counties and organized July 13, 1846.

Judicial District.

Criminal Judicial District.

Civil Judicial Districts 14 and 44.

U. S. Judicial District, Northern.

Senatorial District, 6.

Representative Districts, 73-74.

Congressional District 6.

TERMS OF COURT.

U. S. Circuit and District Courts (Northern District), meets at Dallas 2d Monday in Jan. and 3rd Monday in May.

Meets at Waco 2d Monday in April and 3rd Monday in November.

Meets at Graham 2d Monday in March and 3rd Monday in October.

OFFICERS OF U. S. CIRCUIT & DIST. COURTS.

Circuit Judges { Don A. Pardee, New Orleans, La. / A. P. McCormick, Dallas, Texas.

District Judge............John B. Rector, Dallas, Texas.

District Attorney......W. O. Hamilton, Comanche, Tex.

U. S. Marshall....................P. B. Hunt. Dallas, Tex

U. S. Clerk... ....J. H. Finks, Waco, Tex.

Deputy Clerks { Chas. H. Lednum, Dallas, Tex. / F. W. Giraud, Graham, Texas. / C. A. Richardson, Waco, Texas.

U. S. Commissioner.... Chas. H. Lednum, Dallas, Tex.

SUPREME COURT.

Chief Justice....... ....J. F. Brown

Associate Justices, Reuben R. Gaines and L. G. Denman

Clerk....................................Chas. S. Morse

Court sits at Austin from first Monday in October to last Saturday in following June.

Dallas Term—First Monday in January in each year, and may continue until the last day of March thereafter, unless the business before it is sooner disposed of.

Tyler Term—First Monday in October in each year, and may continue until the last day of December thereafter, unless the business before it is sooner disposed of.

Austin Term—First Monday in April in each year, and may continue until the last day of June thereafter, unless the business before it is sooner disposed of.

DISTRICT COURTS.

14th Judicial District of Texas.—Terms begin second Mondays in March, May, September and December. R. E. BURKE, Judge.

44th Judicial District of Texas.—Terms begin first Mondays in January, April, June and October. EDWARD GRAY, Judge.

CRIMINAL DISTRICT COURT.

Terms begin first Monday in January, April, July and October. CHAS. F. CLINT. Judge.

COUNTY COURT.

Terms begin first Mondays in January, March, May, July, September and November.

THOS. F. NASH, Judge.

COMMISSIONERS' COURT.

Regular Terms second Mondays in February, May, August and November.

Call Terms second Mondays in January, March, April, June, July. September, October and December.

COURT OF CIVIL APPEALS.

FIRST DISTRICT (GALVESTON).

Chief Justice....................C. C. Garrett

Associate Justices { F. A. Williams, H. C. Pleasants,

Clerk.........................H. M. Knight

SECOND DISTRICT (FT. WORTH).

Chief Justice ....B. D. Tarlton

Associate Justices, I. W. Stephens & H. O. Head

Clerk...........................W. L. Huff

THIRD DISTRICT (AUSTIN).

Chief Justice.................. ...H. C. Fisher

Associate Justices, W. E. Collard & W. M. Key

Clerk................ ....Will L Vining.

FOURTH DISTRICT (SAN ANTONIO).

Chief Justice..................Jno. H. James

Associate Justices.....H. H. Neill & W. S. Fly

Clerk.......................H. E. Hildebrand

FIFTH DISTRICT (DALLAS).

Chief Justice.............Henry W. Lightfoot

Associate Justices { Anson Rainey N. W. Finley

Clerk........................Geo. W. Blair

The terms of said Courts shall commence on the first Monday in September of each year, and may continue in session until the first Monday in July of each succeeding year.

COURT OF CRIMINAL APPEALS.

Presiding Judge..................J. M. Hurt
Judges....W. L. Davidson. & E. J. Simpkins
Asst. Atty. General.............R. L. Henry
Court Stenographer.... ....J. B. Earle
Clerk at Tyler..................E. P. Smith
Clerk at Dallas........... ....W. A. Hudson
Clerk at Austin..................P. Walton

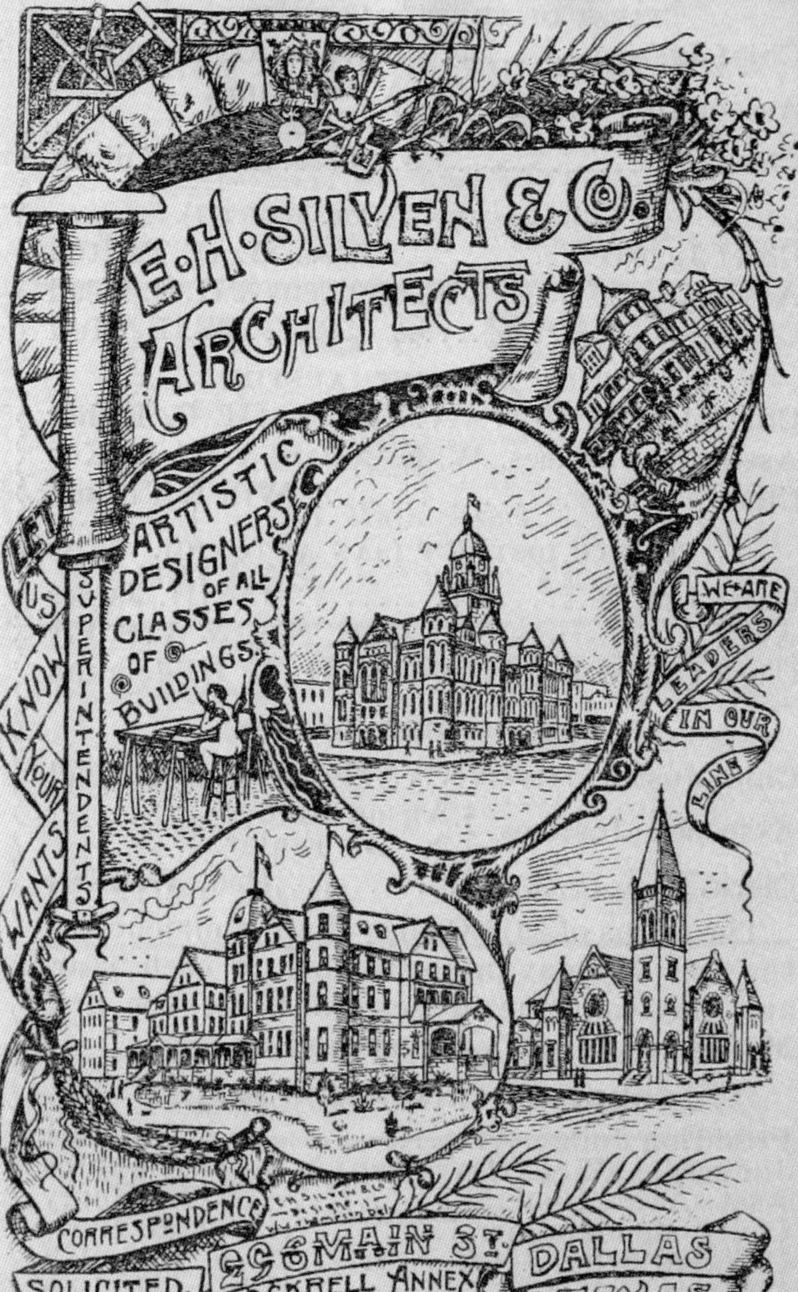
E. H. SILVEN & CO.
ARCHITECTS
ARTISTIC DESIGNERS OF ALL CLASSES OF BUILDINGS.
LET US KNOW YOUR WANTS
SUPERINTENDENTS
WE ARE LEADERS IN OUR LINE
CORRESPONDENCE SOLICITED.
MAIN ST.
COCKRELL ANNEX BUILDING.
DALLAS TEXAS.

Farming and Stock Raising.

FARMING and stock-raising combined is a paying business in Dallas County. While farming alone is very profitable on account of the varied crops that can be raised and which mature at different seasons of the year, and the good markets within easy reach, growing cattle or hogs, or both, can be carried on well at the same time, and by feeding straw, corn or cotton seed to stock in a country where climate and nature alone does so much toward developing an animal; good cattle and hogs can be produced cheaply and taken without expense to a home market at the Dallas stock yards and packing houses and sold at good prices. A good market is here established for cattle, hogs, sheep, horses and mules.

Owing to the native pasturage the year through, and the mild winters and small expense of raising, they can be produced and fattened for market 25 per cent. cheaper than in any state, and 50 per cent. cheaper than in many states, and it can be established as a fact that 50 bushels of corn will finish and fatten a steer in Texas as well as 80 bushels in the latitude of Chicago and Omaha.

Dallas county has no superior for the rearing of fine horses.

There are several such stock farms in the county and all report a most prosperous business. Dallas County is the home of Lena Hill. two year-old; race record 2:12¾, which hold the race record of the world.

I WANT..

...TO TRADE!...

..DO YOU?

C. H. Alexander,

Real Estate

DALLAS, . . . TEXAS.

FARM PRODUCTS FOR THE YEAR 1893, DALLAS COUNTY.

There are 1391 farms in the county, 931 renters on farms, 647 farm laborers employed on the farms during the year.

	Acres.	Products.	Value.
Cotton	63,727	39,806 b.	$1,077,452
Corn	47,254	1,389,099 bu.	433,107
Wheat	19,185	287,578 bu.	137,962
Oats	21,652	654,54 bu.	1514,984
Barley	184	2,184 bu.	775
Rye	67	1,600 bu.	565
Sweet Potatoes	273	18,105 bu.	9,862
Irish Pocatoes	69½	3,041 bu.	1,845
Peas	4½	144 bu.	135
Beans	2	65 bu.	55
Cultivatsd Hay	785	1,433 tons	14,369
Prairie Hay	4,126	63,942 tons	24,077
Millett	284	463 tons	2,691
Sugar Cane	6	6 bbls.	130
Sorghum Cane	142	211 bbls.	2,585
Peaches	26	860 bu.	430
Plums	6	....	230
Pears	2	....	25
Mellons	101	....	2,475
Garden	142	....	6,305
Grapes	91	....	735
Bees	2,433 st'nds,	46,800 lbs.	5,145

MISCELLANEOUS VALUES.

	Number.	Value.
Horses and Mules	20,862	$781,185
Cattle	27,220	199,785
Sheep	5,253	6,815
Goats	663	505
Hogs	15,845	41,880

A large number of farmers refused to make reports on the blanks furnished, and as the assessor made up his statement from statistics given in by the farmers, he only counted those reporting.

COUNTY STATEMENT.

Rate of tax (County) on the $100.00 valuation for 1894, is 55 cents. On February 1, 1894, the balance in the county treasury, was $57,-024.80.

Bonds Redeemed during 1893	$44.500 00
Grand Jury and Grand Jury Baliffs	3.877 00
For Petit Jurors	21.393 50
Net Income for 1893	$186.390.40
Amt. Court House bonds outstg. Feb. 1, 1894	315.000.00
Amt. Jail bonds outstg. Feb. 1. 1894	30.000.00
Amt. road & bridge bonds outstg. Feb. 1, 1894	20.000.00

Dallas County now levies an advalorum tax of 15 cents on each $100.00 worth of property for road and bridge purposes. To the amount thus collected is added the fines and forfeitures collected in the various courts of the county, making a total road and bridge fund of $48,419.14 taking last year as an average. There is now pending before the people a proposition to be rated on August 4th, to determine whether or not the Commissioners' Court shall levy an additional 15 cents on the $100.00 worth of property, making a total of 30 cents. If this proposition should carry it will give the county about $80,000 annually for road and bridge purposes. This amount judiciously expended for five years will give Dallas County a system of publie roads equal to any in the United States.

Wheat Harvest Calendar.

Wheat is harvested in the different countries in the following months.

JANUARY:—Australia, New Zealand, Chili and Argentine Republic.

FEBRUARY AND MARCH:—Upper Egypt and India.

APRIL:—Lower Egypt, India, Syria, Cyprus, Persia, Asia Minor, Mexico and Cuba.

MAY:—*Texas*, Algeria, Central Asia, China, Japan and Morocco.

JUNE:—California, Oregon, Missippippi, Alabama, Georgia, Kentucky, North Carolina, South Carolina, Tennessee, Virginia, Kansas, Arkansas, Utah, Colorado, Missouri, Turkey, Greece, Italy, Spain and South of France.

JULY:—New England, New York, Pennsylvania, Ohio, Indiana, Michigan, Illinois, Iowa, Wisconsin, Southern Minesota, Nebraska, Upper Canada, Roumainia, Bulgaria, Austria, Hungary, South of Russia, Germany, Switzerland and South of England.

AUGUST:—Central and Northern Minnesota, the Dakotas, Manitoba, Lower Canada, Columbia and Belgium, Holland, Great Britian, Denmark, Polland and Central Russia.

SEPTEMBER AND OCTOBER:—Scotland, Sweeden, Norway and North of Russia.

NOVEMBER:—Peru and South Africa.

DECEMBER: — Burmah and New South Wales.

Distances from Various Cities of the World to Dallas.

Place	Miles
Abiline, Tex., via. T & P Ry	191
Austin, Tex	220
Brownville, Tex., via. T & P Ry	563
Bowie, Tex., via. F W & D and T & P Rys	123
Corpus Christi, Tex	418
Decatur, Tex. via. F W & D C Ry	67
El Paso, Tex., via. T & P Ry	647
Ft. Worth, Tex., via. T & P Ry	32
Galveston, Tex., via. Santa Fe Ry	314
Houston, Tex., via. Santa Fe Ry	264
Henrietta, Tex	127
Laredo. Tex., via. Santa Fe	454
Longview. Tex	124
Marshall, Tex., via T & P	147
McKinney, Tex	32
Minneola, Tex., via. T & P	78
Paris, Tex., via. Santa Fe	99
San Antonio, Tex. via. Santa Fe	301
Sierra Blanca, Tex., via. T & P	556
Terrell, Tex., via. T & P	32
Texarkana, Tex., via. T & P	221
Tyler, Tex., via. T & P	103
Vernon, Tex., via. F W & D C	195
Weatherford, Tex., via. T & P	63
Wichita Falls, Tex., via. F W & D C	156
Little Rock, via. T. & P	366
Chattanooga, Tenn., via. T & P	856
Memphis, Tenn., via. T & P	518
Chicago, Ill., via. T & P	994
Cincinnatti, Ohio, via. T & P	1,023
Denver, Col., via. F W & D C	837
Kansas City, Mo., via. Santa Fe	485
New Orleans, La., via. T & P	514
St. Louis, Mo	711
Springfield, Ill	809
New York City	1,745
San Francisco, Cal	1,933
Capetown, via. London	12,952
Hong Kong, via. San Francisco	9,474
Paris, via. New York	5,745
City of Mexico	1,303

No Gold — **No Mineral**

The Dallas Ensor Institute

FOR THE CURE OF

Liquor, Morphine, Cocaine and Tobacco Habits

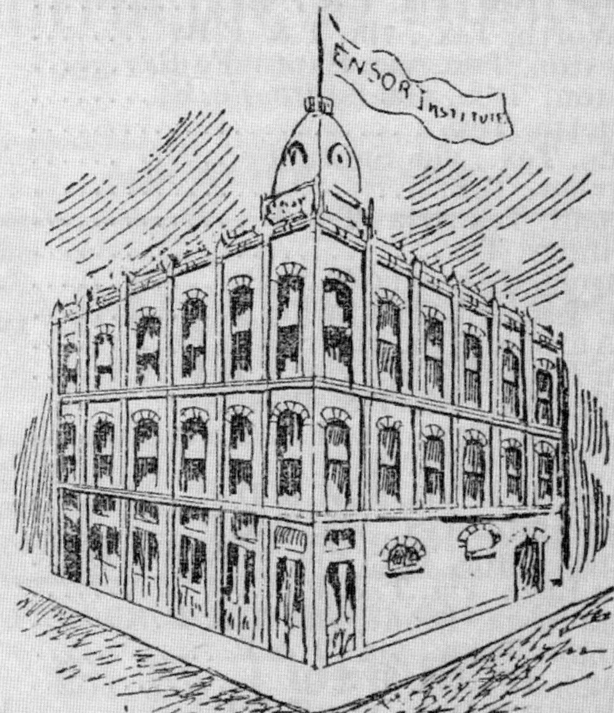

No. 287 Elm Street,

Opened in the City of Dallas on the 1st day of July, 1893, and has successfully cured **Two Hundred and Sixty-Three people** all told, who are to-day sober men with the exception of three.

We Guarantee a Cure in every case, to the entire satisfaction of the patient, or it COSTS HIM NOTHING.

REMEMBER, NO CURE, NO PAY.

Consultation Free and Correspondence Solicited.

Address Lock Box 367.

C. B. BEARD, Manager.

CALL AND SEE US

COME TO TEXAS.

The "Lone Star" is waving—the flag of the free—
Then strike for Texas, if men you would be.
No idlers are wanted, the thrifty and wise.
To wealth and high station can equally rise.

Where corn, oats and cotton; the richest of loam
Which yields to the settler provisions and home.
Trees, of every description arise on each hand.
From alluvial soil to the rich table land.

Here springs are exhaustless, and streams never dry,
In the season from winter to autumn's bright sky,
A wide panorama of prairie is seen:
Of grasses of all kinds perennially green

Here millions of cattle, sheep, horses and goats
Grow fat as if stall-fed or fattened on oats.
No poverty is found in the mighty domain,
To the man who exerts either finger or brain.

Here are homes for the millions, the rich and the poor,
While Texas opens wide her hospitable door.
She has thousands of acres—yes, millions to sell.
Yet can point without cost, to where pre-emptors can dwell.
Her terms will be easy with those whom she deals
While security, all, in their title can feel.

Buy land while 'tis cheap, and the finest select,
'Twill, young men, prove a fortune when least, you expect.
Old man, for your children, buy, file it away:
A God-send 'twill prove on some rainy day.

THE STANDARD MARKET,

107 ERVAY STREET.

The Pioneer Butcher, C. H. WILLIAMS,

Wholesale and Retail Dealer in

Fresh and Salt Meats, Sea and Lake Fish

LIVE AND DRESSED POULTRY.
VEGETABLES AND GAME IN SEASON.

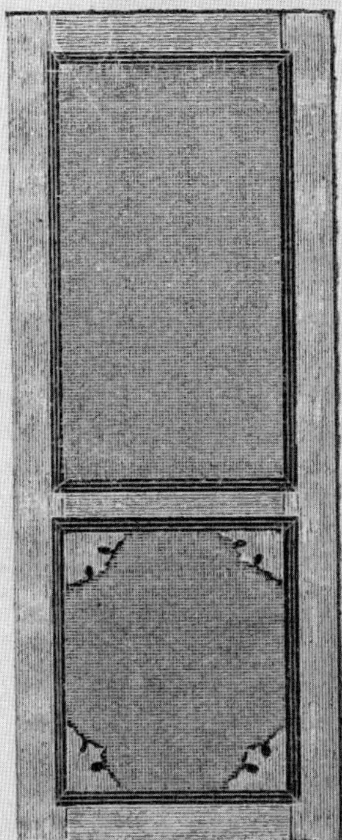

We Manufacture

SCREENS

EXCLUSIVELY.

All Grades, from the CHEAPEST to the FINEST.

Our Screens cannot be Excelled either in Price or Quality.

DON'T FAIL TO GET OUR PRICES.

DALLAS SCREEN CO.

Corner Ross Avenue and North Akard Sts.

Wiley Perry. D. C. Holland.

Perry & Holland,

Blacksmithing,

HORSE SHOEING AND GENERAL REPAIRING,

493 Elm Street, DALLAS, TEXAS.

LOCATION OF FIRE ALARM BOXES.

4 Carondelet and Market (Engine House No. 1.)
5 Commerce and Hawkins (Engine House No. 2.)
6 Bryan, near Crocket
7 Main and Harwood (Chemical Engine No. 1.)
8 Gaston and College (Engine House No. 3.)
9 Bullington & Cottage Lane (Private.)
12 Houston and Columbia
13 Houston and Commerce
14 Austin and Commerce
15 Market and Wood
16 Lamar and Elm
17 Lamar and Young
18 Jefferson and Elm
19 Poydras and Jackson
21 Akard and Elm
23 Lamar and Cochran
24 Griffin and Collin
25 Griffin and Elm
26 Main and Martin
27 Akard and Patterson ave
28 Akard and Ross Ave.
31 Ross Ave. and Magnolia
32 Commerce and Akard H. & L. Cent. Station.
34 Lacy and Wood
35 Akard and Young
36 Akard and Canton
37 Ervay and Jackson
38 Lamar St. and Santa Fe
39 Cotton Compress Co. (Private.)
41 Ervay and Park
42 Browder and Corsicana
43 Evergreen and St. Louis
45 Pocahontas & Harwood
46 Williams and Harwood
51 Wood and Harwood
52 Elm and Ervay
53 Bryan and Masten
54 Orange and Cochran
61 Caroline and McK. Ave
62 Caroline and Ashland
63 Harwood and McK. Ave.
64 Caruth and Masten
68 Payne and Highland
71 Ross Ave. and Pearl
72 Harwood & San Jacinto
73 Leonard & San Jacinto
81 Boll and San Jacinto
82 Preston & Commerce
61 Main and Field
92 Griffin and Camp
123 Holmes and Forest Ave.
124 Main and Lloyd
125 Elm and Hawkins
126 Pearl and Live Oak
127 Elm and Olive
132 Elm St. & Trunk Ry.
134 Main and Duncan
155 Williams and Crowdus
212 Floyd and Cantegral
213 Live Oak & Cantegral
214 Lake and Hunt
215 Pearl & Cottage Lane
232 Leonard and Flora
234 Preston & Pacific Ave.
235 Germania and San J.
236 Bryan and Germania
237 Greenwood and Oak
238 Gibbs and Griffin
241 Howard Oil Mills (Gen. Alarm Private)
242 Ross Ave. and Hall St.
243 Ross and Wash. Ave.
245 Live Oak and Adair
246 Expo. Ave. and Santa Fe
247 Worth and Wash. Ave.
248 Race and Wash. Ave.
251 Swiss and Wash. Ave.
253 Gaston & Haskell
256 Swiss Ave. and Peak St.
261 Bryan and Annex
312 Preston and Eakin
314 Park and Gano
315 Hughes and Ervay
316 Akard and Pocahontas
317 Beaumont and Browder
318 Corinth and Ervay
321 Corinth and Cockrell
323 Ervay and Grand Ave.
324 Hickory and Central Ry
412 Washington & Thomas
413 McK. and Maple Ave
415 McKinney and Boll
416 Howell and Peak
521 Allen and Juliette
424 Hall and Central Ry.
426 McK. and Lemmon

SIGNALS.

Three times 3 strokes, 2d alarm; 3 times 6 strokes, general alarm; 3 single strokes fire under control; 1 single stroke at 12 m., noon drill; 1 single stroke at 9 p.m. evening drill; 9 a. m and 3 p. m., two strokes, test of line.

ALL STEEL. WILL LAST FOREVER.

Why slobber your corn and cotton all over the field when the **New Empress** puts it down like clockwork With this Planter you can plant almost any kind of seed, such as Corn, Cotton, Sorghum, Peas and Beans, with perfect accuracy.

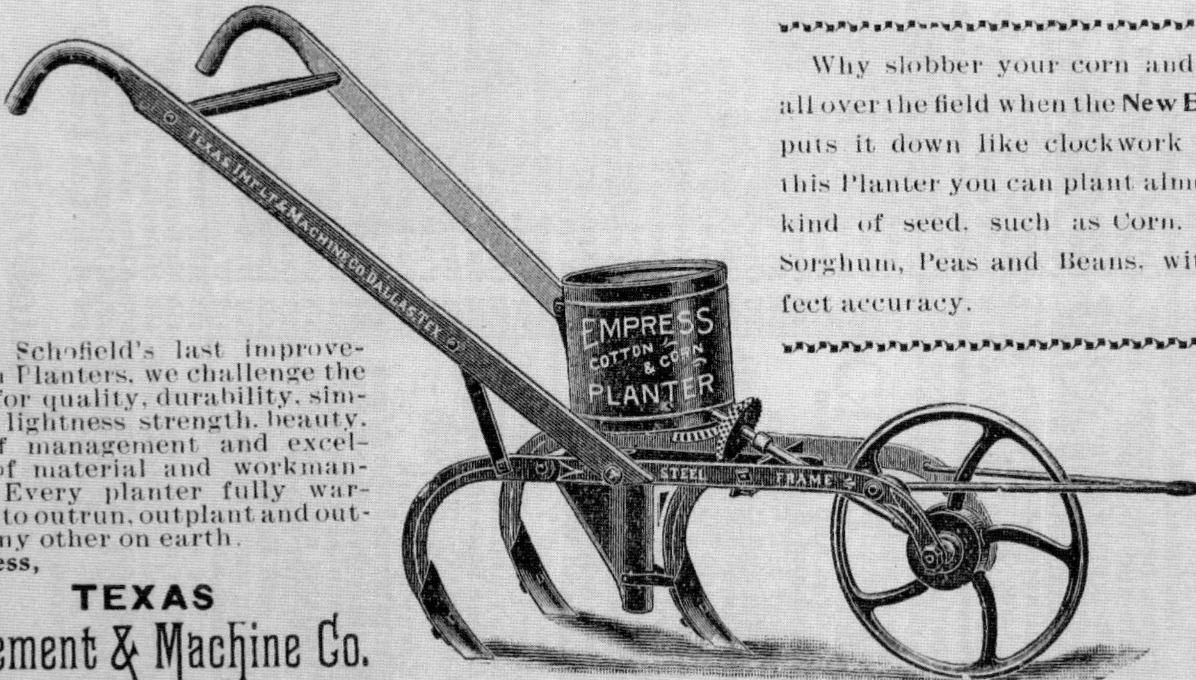

With Schofield's last improvement in Planters, we challenge the world for quality, durability, simplicity, lightness strength, beauty, ease of management and excellence of material and workmanship. Every planter fully warranted to outrun, outplant and outwear any other on earth.

Address,

TEXAS

Implement & Machine Co.

DALLAS, TEXAS.

LIGHTNING CALCULATOR.

Pounds of Cotton.

Price Per Hundred

0	1	2	3	4	5	6	7	8	9	10	20	30	40	50	60	70	80	90	100
50	0	1	1	2	2	3	3	4	4	5	10	15	20	25	30	35	40	45	50
55	1	1	2	2	3	3	4	4	5	5½	11	16½	22	27½	33	38½	44	49½	55
60	1	1	2	2	3	4	4	5	5	6	12	18	24	30	36	42	48	54	60
65	1	1	2	3	3	4	5	5	6	6½	13	19½	26	32½	39	45½	52	58½	65
70	1	1	2	3	3	4	5	6	6	7	14	21	28	35	42	49	56	63	70
75	1	1	2	3	4	4	5	6	7	7½	15	22½	30	37½	45	52½	60	67½	75
80	1	2	2	3	4	5	6	6	7	8	16	24	32	40	48	56	64	72	80
85	1	2	3	3	4	5	6	7	8	8½	17	25½	34	42½	51	59½	68	76½	85
90	1	2	3	4	4	5	6	7	8	9	18	27	36	45	54	63	72	81	90
95	1	2	3	4	5	6	7	8	9	9½	19	28½	38	47½	57	66½	76	85½	95
100	1	2	3	4	5	6	7	8	9	10	20	30	40	50	60	70	80	90	100

To take from table 953 pounds at 55 cents, 90 pounds is 49½ cents; 900 pounds ten times as much, $4 95 cents; 50 pounds is 27 cents, and 3 pounds 2 cents. Total, $5.24.

Grand . Windsor

.. Hotel ..

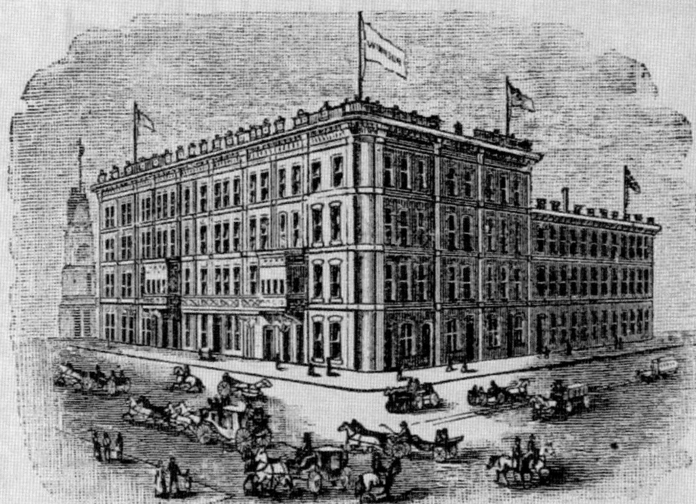

Main, Austin and Commerce Sts.,

DALLAS, - - TEXAS.

This old established and Popular Hotel is situated in the business center of Dallas, and close to all the Railroad Depots. Street Cars from all parts of the City pass the doors every three minutes.

The house is thoroughly equipped with all modern improvements, and is first-class in all its appointments—Elevators, Steam Heating, Artesian Water, Etc.

Rates Reasonable. A. L. HODGE, Propr.

DALLAS A HOTEL CENTER.

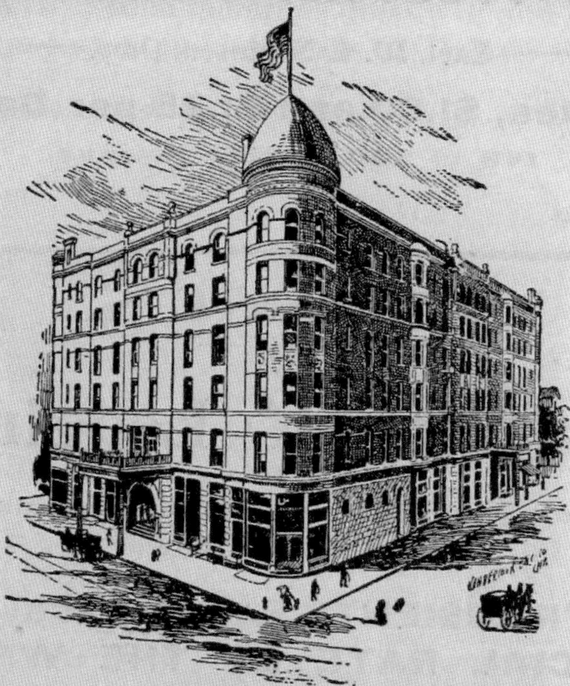

THE ORIENTAL.

"Who'ere has traveled Life's dull round,
Whe're his stages may have been,
May sigh to think he still has found
His warmest welcome at an Inn."

—*Shenstone.*

The stranger coming to Dallas considers before his arrival the prospect of a pleasant stay. Convenience, too, is considered and as Dallas hotels are all centrally located they are convenient both for business and pleasure.

The genialty, hospitality and generous good spirit for which Dallas people are noted, is reflected in the management of these successful hotels.

Look where the traveler will, nowhere will he find such perfect appointments; such splendid service; such generous good will and homelike comfort as in the hotels of Dallas.

✦ ✦ THE MC LEOD HOTEL. ✦ ✦

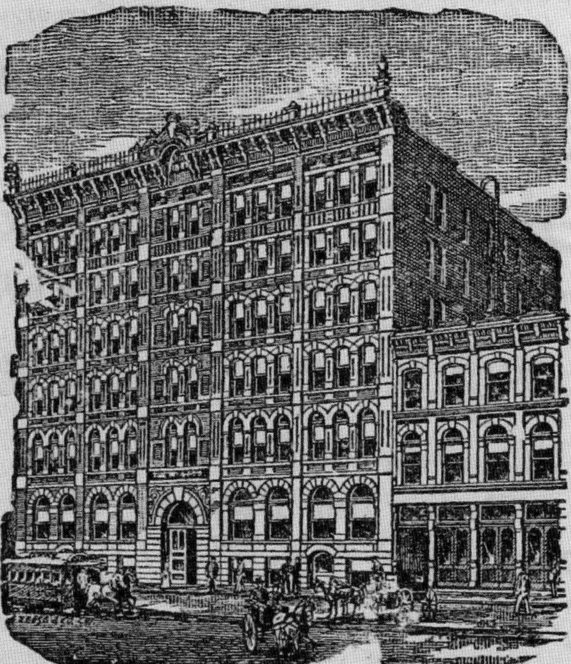

Central location; all modern improvements, and electric lights. Our own Artesian well furnishes the water. Smooth elevator; commodious sample rooms and excellent table. Those who visit us once come again.

N. B. SLIGH, Lessee and Proprietor.

ARLINGTON—337-339 Main St., E. J. Faull, Proprietor.
GRAND WINDSOR—Main & Com. Sts. A L. Hodge, Prop.
McLEOD—317-323 Main Sts. N. B. Sligh, Proprietor.
ORIENTAL—Commerce & Akard Sts., W. J. Alden, Mgr.
PHŒNIX—198-200 Pacific Ave., W. L. Robinson, Prop.
ST. GEORGE—244 Main St., H. K. Brooks, Mgr.
SHUFORD—153 Patterson, Ave., J. Z. T. Shuford, Prop.
ST. JAMES—278 Main St., Thos. McChristy, Proprietor.
There are 25 other Hotels, and 121 Boarding Houses.

DALLAS STREET CAR SERVICE.

The Dallas Consolidated Traction Ry. Co. operates about 10 miles of electric and 16 miles of horse car line. Wm. Dresser, Supt.; Sam P. Cochran, receiver; J. L. Sale, P. A.

Main St., Washington Ave. and Live Oak line starts from court house every 11 minutes. Runs east on Main street to Washington Ave., thence north to Live Oak, where it connects at corner of Washington Ave. and Live Oak street with San Jacinto mule car line, also College line. There are eight cars on the line; four cars going directly up Main street and four cars turn from Main at Preston, going out Swiss Ave. and Live Oak street.

San Jacinto mule car line starts from court house every 11 minutes, and makes connections with above lines as mentioned.

Ervay street mule car line starts at court house, running east on Main to post-office; thence south through the most beautiful portion of our city, passing City Park. Cars every eight minutes.

South Harwood (Belt Line), starts at court house, runs east on Main to post-office, thence south on Ervay to Commerce, thence east on Commerce to South Harwood, thence south to Corinth, thence west to Ervay street stables, at which point it connects with Belt Line proper. Cars every 10 minutes.

Belt Line mule cars pass Sanger Bros. on Lamar street, going north and south, every 12

T. F. RAGLAND,

PRACTICAL

Painter and Decorator

SATISFACTION GUARANTEED.

Office and Shop, 362 Commerce St., DALLAS, TEXAS.

C. B. ANDERSON & CO.

The Pioneer Portrait House of Texas.

ESTABLISHED 1884.

Is to-day better equipped than any house in the Southwest to produce all grades and styles of Portrait Work promptly. We are always in need of reliable Agents, to whom we are ever ready to give the most liberal terms.

We handle all the latest designs in Frames and are prepared to meet the sharpest competition. It will pay every Agent in the South to get our prices on Frames and save large freight bills. If you want something with which to take orders and reap a handsome profit, let us make you a sample of our "AA" grade Crayon work and frame it in our new No. 51 Oak Frame. This is sure to please everybody.

C. B. ANDERSON & CO.,

No. 400 Elm St., DALLAS, TEXAS.

REFERENCES—City National Bank of Dallas, or any Express Company in Dallas.

DALLAS TELEGRAPH COLLEGE

Guild Building, 369 Elm Street,

Established 1889. DALLAS, TEXAS.

The most Practical School of Telegraphy in the United States. Owns and operates a main line 6 miles in length. Pupils do actual business for the public. Pupils wanted. For terms, etc., address

L. C. ROBINSON, Principal.

minutes. This line also runs through some of the most beautiful resident streets. The Consolidated Company is prepared to move from 1200 to 1500 people in a body.

The Dallas & Oak Cliff Elevated Ry. Trains leave Dallas on Commerce street every 15 minutes, from 6:30 a. m. until 11:30 p. m. daily, on and after September 1, 1894.

The Dallas Rapid Transit Ry. consists of a six-mile belt, extending from the Opera House and Windsor Hotel, corner Commerce and Austin streets, east on Commerce street to Exposition avenue, thence to the grounds of the Texas State Fair and Dallas Exposition, continuing around by South Park, Edgewood Place, Chestnut Hill and Cotton Mills to Opera House and Tabernacle. The Preston street belt, about 1½ miles long, branches from main belt on Commerce, at Preston street, continuing southeast, connecting with main line at South Park. Belt cars going in opposite directions, leaves the opera house on the even hour and half hour, and again cars going on Commerce street at 15 minutes past each hour.

The Queen City Railway Company's Elm street cars start from Commerce and Houston streets over Commerce to Market, thence to Elm, then all the way out Elm street past the Union Depot to the Texas State Fair and Dallas Exposition grounds. These cars run every seven minutes. Pearl street cars start from Houston & Elm out Elm to Ervay, out Live Oak Pearl, then northward to McKinney avenue. These cars run every 20 minutes, leaving each end on the half hour, 10 minutes before and 10 minutes after the hour.

W. H. HATCH,

WHOLESALE

Agricultural Implements

BUGGIES, PHAETONS, HACKS AND CARTS,

113 and 115 Jefferson Street,

136, 138 140 and 142 Elm St.,

DALLAS, - - TEXAS.

J. W. Slaughter. G. I. Mottwiler.

Slaughter & Mottwiler

Contractors ....and.... Builders.

Plans Furnished,

Work Superintended,

362 Commerce Street, Dallas, Texas.

The New Capitol Building of Texas.

★ ★ ★

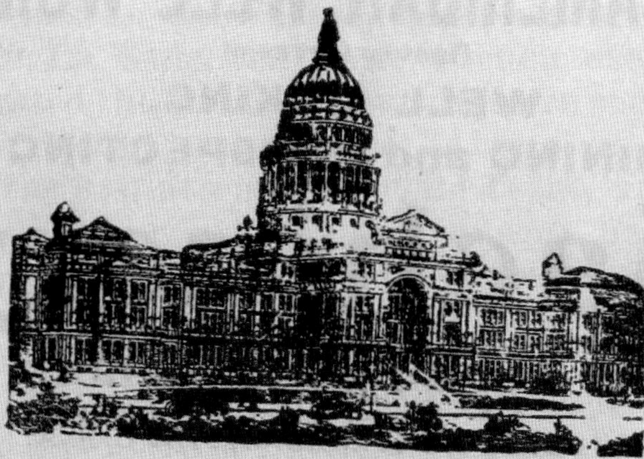

LOCATED AT AUSTIN.

DESCRIPTION.

The building is a fire-proof structure, classic in design. Its form approximates a Greek cross with projecting center and flanks; rotunda and dome at the intersection of the main corridors. It is 556 feet 6 inches long, inclusive of porticos, and 288 feet 10 inches at its greatest width: it is 311 feet in height from grade line to top of statute on dome. Besides the basement and dome elevation it is three full stories in height.

It has perfect apparatus for lighting the building by electricity, steam heating, ventilating, plumbing, drainage, sewerage, hydraulic elevators, and all other appliances and conveniences of a modern state capital.

Largest capital building of any state in the Union. It is only second in size to the capital at Washington, and is the seventh largest building in the world.

TEXAS IN BRIEF.

TEXAS is supposed to have derived its name from a small tribe of Indians of the village Tehas, on the Neches, signifiing "friend." In 1680, La Salle, the great French explorer, penetrated this immense southwestern country. On the part of the Spanish, Alonzo de Leon made the first attempt to settle Texas, and in 1691 a governor and troops were sent here by Spain. La Salle called the country Louisiana, for Louis XIV. The Spaniards named it New Philippines, in honor of Phillip V. San Antonio, the oldest European settlement in Texas, was founded in 1693; Goliad and Nacogdoches in 1717. The foundation of the Alamo was laid in 1744, and was denominated a mission.

Prior to 1820 Texas was ruled by governors. In 1823, Stephen F. Austin arrived with colonists, when the Mexican States of Coahuila and Texas were constituted one government, with their capital at Saltillo. Complaints of failure by these to the Mexican government finally eventuated in the revolution of 1835. On march 2, 1836, Texas declared itself a free and independent government, adopting a constitution on the 17th of the same month. The first president was David G. Burnet. Gen. Sam Houston was made commander-in-chief of the Texan forces, and after terrible fights and struggles, the heroic band, only one-third in number of their enemies, gained the decisive battle of San Jacinto, on April 21. 1836. Texas's annexation to the United States took place in 1845. The State seceeded from the Union

Walker China Hall,

CHINA and
...GLASSWARE...

Cut Glass, Bric-a-Brac

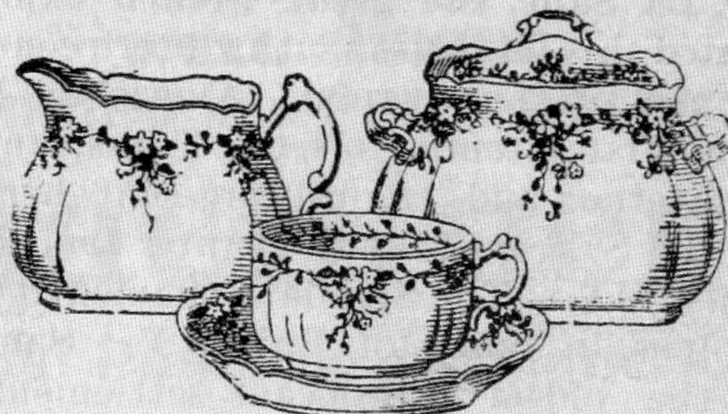

and Fancy China.

Open Stock Decorated China Dinner Ware—Buy as much or little as you want, until set is complete.

J. B. CUMMINS, PROPRIETOR,

248 ELM STREET. DALLAS, TEXAS.

CANCER

DR. W. N. JONES

Never Fails to CURE

No Poison Used.

. . . NO KNIFE.

Cancers,
Rodent Ulcers
and Tumors.

Hundreds Cured.

MY MOTTO: NO CURE, NO PAY.

OFFICE, Moore Block, South Side Square,

SHERMAN, - - - TEXAS.

February 1, 1861. In 1870 it was re-admitted.

Texas is the largest state in the Union, being six times larger than New York, seven times as large as Ohio, and 100,000 square miles larger than all of the Eastern and Middle states, including Deleware and Maryland. Compared with the countries of Europe, it has 34,000 square miles more than the Austrian Empire, 62,000 more than the German Empire, and nearly 70,000 square miles more than France.

Texas is 825 miles long and 740 miles wide, containing an area of 274,356 square miles.

TEXAS PRODUCTS.

	Value.
Cotton, 2,025,066 bales, $35 per bale,	$70,877,310
Cotton seed, 900,000 tons..........	15,500,000
Wheat, 10,000,000 bu..............	5,200,000
Corn, 64,000,000 bu................	32,000,000
Oats, 25,000,000 bu................	7,500,000
Orchard Fruits....................	3,000,000
Garden Products...................	3,000,000
Sugar..............................	1,200,000
Syrup..............................	200,000
Sweet Potatoes.....................	1,700,000
Irish Potatoes.....................	860,000
Cattle, 7,000,000..................	84,000,000
Horses, 1,200,000..................	42,000,000
Sheep, 4,334,551...................	8,669,102
Hogs, 3,500,000....................	12,000,000
Manufactured Products..............	37,000,000
Bees and Poultry...................	3,000,000
Rye, Barley, Buckwheat and Wool.	3,200,000
Total............................	$331,106,412

The official estimate for 1892 was $323,430,000.

The various products will be nearly double this year.

Texas will soon be able to feed the world.

MODEL ✦ BAKERY,

CHAS. GOODMAN, Proprietor.

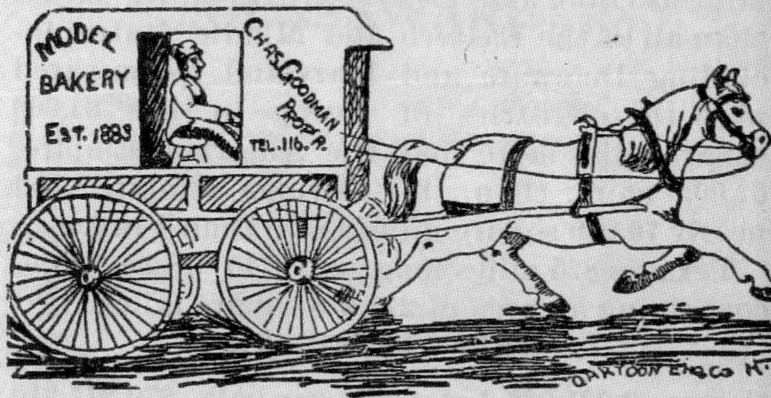

A SPECIALTY:

Country Merchants Supplied with FRESH BREAD AND CAKES DAILY

Telephone 116. **377 Elm Street, Dallas.**

BRANCH STORE, 298 Main Street.

"ALWAYS ON TIME."

Dallas Transfer & Cab Co.

Will Furnish Carriage. Bus or Baggage Wagon for any kind of work in their respective lines,

Will Shoe your Horse, Repair, Paint or Build all kinds of Vehicles.

TRANSFER OFFICE, 144 South Ervay Street.
REPAIR SHOPS, 433 Jackson Street,

Telephone No. 52. Dallas, Texas.

The Mineral Resources of Texas.

THE rapid advancement made by Texas up to the present time has been based almost entirely upon her agricultural resources, and is due to the remarkable fertility of many of her soils and to the great variety of products derived from their cultivation.

To-day another field opens, and she spreads before the world her wealth of mineral resources, which if they do not exceed those of agricultural promise to equal them in all respects.

The attention of capitalists, both home and foreign, is being directed to these fields, and the sinking of mines, and the erection of furnaces and factories for the recovery and utilization of the various metals and other materials occuring here are already in progress.

Iron, petroleum, copper, lead, gypsum, potters clay, fire clay and kaolin, hydraulic limestone and cement materials, greensand marls, glass sands, building stones and marbles, natural gas, salt, manganese, gold, and silver. In addition are valuable deposits of asphaltum, bat guano, millstone grit, marls, lithographic stone, soapstone and other minerals.

TIMBER SUPPLY.

There were 164 varieties of Texas woods shown at the New Orleans Exposition. The entire Eastern region of the state is a forest of pine, oak, walnut, ash, and cedar. Cypress and pecán, hickory, gum, cottonwood and elm are found in most all parts of the state in the river valleys.

Queen City Dye Works

Practical Steam Cleaners and Dyers of

SILK, STIFF AND SOFT HATS.

Garments of all kinds Cleaned and Dyed in all Colors.
Repairing, Rebinding and Relining Neatly Done.
ALL WORK GUARANTEED.

J. D. ELLIS, Proprietor,

370 Elm Street, . . . DALLAS, TEXAS.

◆ ◆ THE ◆ ◆

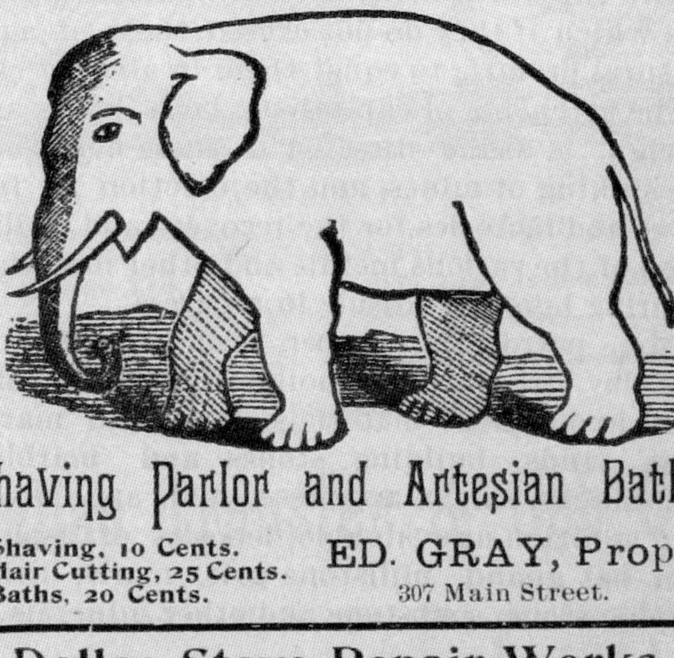

Shaving Parlor and Artesian Baths.

Shaving, 10 Cents.
Hair Cutting, 25 Cents.
Baths, 20 Cents.

ED. GRAY, Prop.,
307 Main Street.

Dallas Stove Repair Works.

Gasoline and all other Stoves.
Wood Stoves Changed to Coal Stoves.

135 North Akard St.,
DALLAS, TEXAS.

E. A. DeMAY, Proprietor.

Texas Pattern & Model Works,

A. GIACOMINI, Proprietor.

MANUFACTURER OF

Small Machinery, Dies, Tools and Artistic Brass Work,

339 Pacific Avenue, Dallas, Texas.

The territory tributary to Dallas, is capable of acommodating comfortably, happily and prosperously, five millions of people, and sustaining in Dallas a manufacturing and commercial population of half a million. We know that Texas is the land of prosperity, progress and promise. It is large enough to sustain a population of fifty million people. As yet, it has but 2,500.000, but the rate is increasing at the rate of 500 to 1000 daily, generally the very best classes of native and foreign immigrants.

Land is cheap, the climate is perfect, timber and water is abundant, the soil is fertile, the people kind, hospitale, intelligent and progressive, and all who come will receive a cordial welcome.

R. J. HURLEY,

BRICK ✦ CONTRACTOR

AND BUILDER.

PRESSED BRICK FRONTS
A SPECIALTY.

REFERENCE TO ANY ARCHITECT IN THE CITY.

OFFICE, 221 TEXAS STREET.

DALLAS, . . . TEXAS.

T. E. THOMAS,

496 Elm St.,
Dallas, Texas.

Barber Shop.

Dr. J. H. Holsey, D. D. S.

The First Colored Dentist in the City. All kinds of Dental Work Done. Strictly First-Class Low Prices.

497 Main Street, DALLAS, TEXAS.

STAR DYE WORKS,

368 Main Street. J. T. W. HILL, Proprietor.

ALL KIODS OF SECOND HAND CLOTHING BOUGHT AND SOLD.

Cleaning, Dyeing and Repairing

IN ALL COLORS.

Satisfaction Given and Solid Colors Guaranteed.
Hats Cleaned, Dyed and Repaired.

J. T. W. HILL, Proprietor,

368 Main St., Dallas, Texas.

TIME TABLE

✦ TEXAS & PACIFIC RAILWAY. ✦

T. & P. R. R. SCHEDULE, AUGUST 26, 1894.

BRICK DEPOT. DALLAS.

EAST-BOUND.		WEST-BOUND.	
No. 2 Leaves	9:30 a. m	No. 1 Leaves	6:30 p. m
No. 4 "	8:10 p. m	No. 3 "	7:48 a. m
No. 6 "	7:20 a. m	No. 5 "	9:25 p. m
No 8 Arrives	11:50 a. m	No. 7 "	3:55 a. m
No. 10 "	5:25 p. m	No. 9 "	1:50 p. m

☞ East-bound trains leave Union Depot. East Dallas. 10 minutes later than Brick Depot, and west-bound 10 minutes earlier.

No. 6, "The St. Louis Limited." (T. & P. Ry.) leaves Dallas at 7:30 a. m. daily, arrives in St. Louis next morning making connections with the "Chicago Limited" from St. Louis to Chicago, a Pullman vestibuled train, leaving St. Louis at 8:45 a. m. same day over the Chicago & Alton railway.

The "St. Louis Limited" of the Texas & Pacific Ry., also makes connections with the "Royal Blue Flyer" of the B. & O. S. W., running solid vestibuled trains to New York.

B. & O. S. W. R. R. CONDENSED SCHEDULE.

Leave	St. Louis, via. B. & O. S. W. R. R.	8:00 a. m
Arrive	Louisville " "	5:50 p. m
"	Cincinnati " "	5:30 p. m
"	Parkersburg, via. B. & O. R. R.	12:50 a. m
"	Cumberland, Eastern Time	7:33 a. m
"	Washington.	11:50 a. m
"	Baltimore.	12:50 p. m
"	Philadelphia, 24th & Chestnut Sts.	3:25 p. m
"	Trenton	5:30 p. m
"	Newark	6:11 p. m
"	New York, foot of Liberty St.	6:15 p. m

✦ DALLAS TIME TABLES. ✦

GULF, COLORADO & SANTA FE R. R.

NORTH-BOUND.	SOUTH-BOUND.
No. 74 Ar ....9:55 a.m	No. 71 Lv..........7:35 a.m
No. 74 Lv...........2:00 p.m	No. 73 Ar..........1:10 p.m
No. 72 Ar..........9:25 p.m	No. 73 Lv ....6:15 p.m

The "Red Express," No. 73 and 74, the new night train on the Santa Fe, makes the quickest time between North and South Texas; also runs a solid vestibuled train between Galveston and St. Louis. The Santa Fe line is the only road running direct from Dallas to Galveston.

W. A. TULEY, T. P. A., Dallas, Tex. W. S. KEENAN, G. P. A., Galveston, Tex.

WALTER G. WILKINS, City Ticket Agt., 182 Main St.' corner Grand Windsor Hotel.

HOUSTON & TEXAS CENTRAL R. R.

NORTH-BOUND.

No. 13 News Train.......................... leaves 4:30 a.m
No. 3 arrives..........................9:35 a.m; leaves 9:50 a.m
No. 1 arrives..........................6:40 p.m; leaves 7:00 p.m

SOUTH-BOUND.

No. 2 arrives.......................... 9:20 a.m; leaves 9:35 a.m
No. 4 arrives.......................... 6:15 p.m; leaves 6:40 p.m
No. 13 arrives.......................10:40 p.m. (News Train.)

MISSOURI, KANSAS & TEXAS R. R.

NORTH-BOUND.

No. 32 arrives....................11:40 a.m.; leaves 11:55 a.m
No. 34 arrives....................10:15 p.m.; leaves 10.30 p.m
No. 16 Henrietta...............................leaves 12:50 p.m
No. 76 Denton Mixed.........................leaves 6:50 p.m
No. 74 Greenville Mixed......................leaves 7:40 a.m

SOUTH-BOUND.

No. 33 arrives .... 6:00 a.m.; leaves 6:20 a.m
No. 31 arrives .... 4:35 p.m.; leaves 4:55 p.m
No. 15 Henrietta................. 2:40 p.m ....
No. 75 Denton Mixed.......... 10:25 a.m ....
No. 91 Hillsboro Mixed.........................leaves 9:35 a.m

TEXAS TRUNK R. R.

Arrives..........10:15 a.m. | Leaves..............4:00 p.m

OUR NEW HEADQUARTERS.

. . THE OLD RELIABLE . .

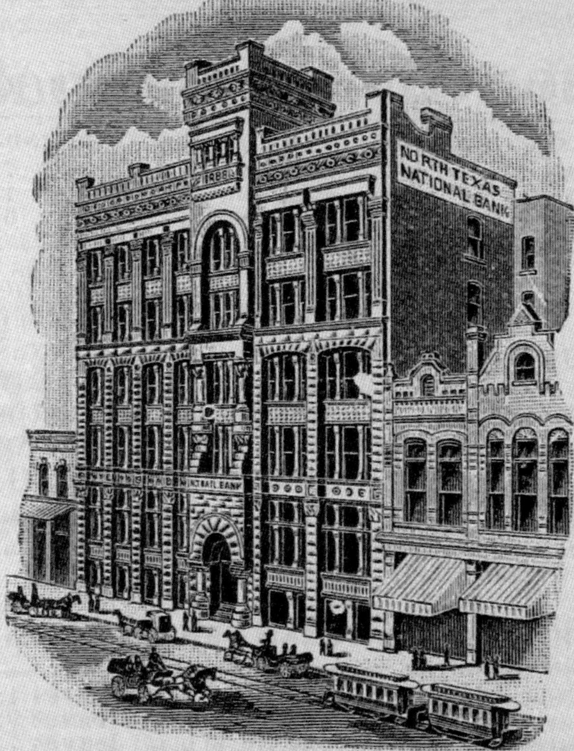

NORTH TEXAS NATIONAL BANK BUILDING.

. . ESTABLISHED 1887 . .

. . THE . .

Dallas Engraving & Mfg. Co.

MANUFACTURERS OF

SUPERIOR RUBBER STAMPS

STENCILS, SEALS, ETC.

Removed to Basement North Texas Bank Building.

If you are in need of anything in our line, call and see us. We can give you the **Best Work at the Lowest Prices. Commercial Printing.**

Telephone 28. Dallas, Texas.

FT. WORTH & DENVER CITY R. R.
(Texas Panhandle Route.)

TIME TABLE AT FT. WORTH.

No. 2 leaves	10:55 a. m.	No. 1 arrives	5:40 p. m
No. 4 "	5:02 p. m.	No. 3 "	10:25 a. m

The shortest and quickest line between Texas and Colorado. 150 to 220 miles saved by this route.

The Fort Worth & Denver City railroad traverses from the Summerland to the Alps. Almost every phase of American scenery—every sharp contrast—from the palms of the South to the heart of the Rockies, can be seen on this road and its connections.

TEXAS MIDLAND R. R.

The Texas Midland Ry. has its headquarters at Terrell, Texas, 31 miles east of Dallas.

The "Midland Route" has extended its line from Roberts to Greenville. In the near future the line (which is in progress) will extend from Greenville to Paris, thence to Hot Springs and Little Rock. It also anticipates extending its line from Ennis to Waco, Austin and San Antonio, then on to the Gulf.

Under its present management this road cannot help but thrive, as its leaders are men of push and energy. In time the Texas Midland route will be the most important railroad line throughout the State of Texas, as it is one of the wealthiest corporations in the Union, and is running through the most fertile and productive sections of the state. It will be but a short time until the "Midland Route" will have a name of world-wide reputation.

Hagey Infirmary

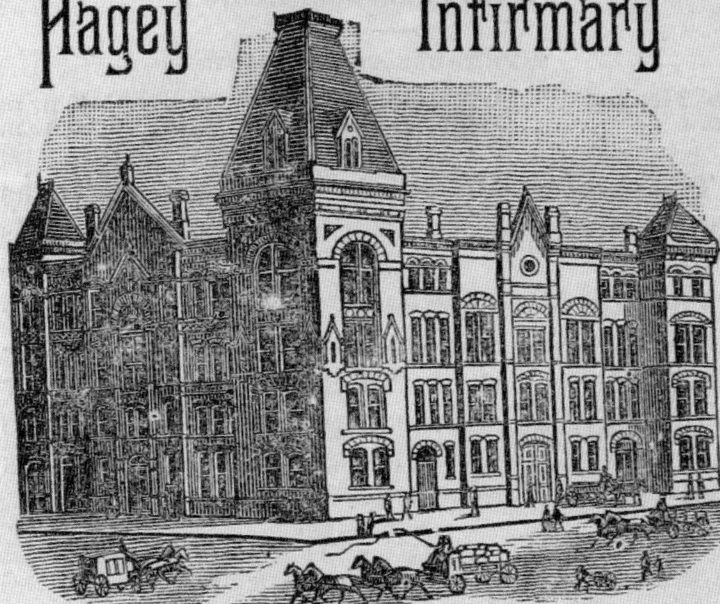

OF DALLAS, TEXAS.

FOR THE CURE OF THE

LIQUOR, MORPHINE, OPIUM,

Cocaine and Tobacco Habits.

No institution in the land is equal to this. The Hagey Remedies are endorsed by thousands of the best people in Texas and other States, and multitudes testify to its efficacy. However frail the patient may be when he enters the institute, he leaves perfectly cured of the habit, with pure blood, strong nerves and restored to health. No disagreeable or bad effects have ever resulted from the treatment. It is absolutely harmless. A cure is guaranteed and accommodation good.

Consultation Free.

Correspondence Solicited.

Morrow Block, Corner Main and Pearl Streets,

DALLAS, TEXAS.

W. F. BALDRIDGE, Manager.

LAWS OF TEXAS.

Referring to Exemptions, Liens Limitations, Etc

Expressly prepared by M. L. Robertson, Esq. of the Dallas Bar.

BILLS AND NOTES.

The liability of a drawer or indorser of a bill of exchange, and endorser of a promisory note may be fixed by protest or by suit at the first term of the court without protest, or by suit at the second term by showing good cause why suit was not brought at first term after right of action accrued.

An assignee of a will may bring suit in his own name.

EXEMPTIONS.

Homestead of a family in city, town or village, shall consist of lot or lots not exceeding in value $5,000 at the time of their designation as the homestead, irrespective of the value of the improvements thereon.

The business homestead is the building or part of building where the head of a family exescises his business or calling, in town or city, shall consist of not more than 200 acres of land which may be in one or two parcels with the improvements thereon, all homestead and kitchen furniture. Any lot or lots in a cemetary for the purpose of sepulture. All implements of husbandry, all tools apparatus and books belonging to any trade or profession. The family library and all family portraits and pictures, live milch cows and their calves. Two yoke of work oxen with necessary yokes and chains, two horses (geldings, mares or mules), and one wagon, one carriage or buggy, one gun.

Twenty hogs, all saddles, bridles and harness necessary for the use of the family. All provisions and forage on hand for home consumption. All current wages for personal services.

FENCES.

A "sufficient fence" must be at least five feet high and hog proof, if it does not come up to these requirements then owner of stock not liable for trespass. Dividing fences can only be renewed by mutual consent or by six months notice in writing prior to removal.

INTEREST.

On all written contracts ascertaining the sum payable when no rate of interest is agreed upon by the parties to the contract, interest shall be allowed at the rate of six per cent. per annum from and after the time when the sum is due and payable. On all open accounts when no rate is fixed by the parties, interest shall be allowed at the rate of six per cent. per annum from the first day of January after the same are made. The parties to any written contract may agree to and stipulate for any rate of interest not exceeding 10 per cent. per annum.

LIENS.

Judgments properly indexed operate as a lien upon real estate when entered upon the judgment record in the county clerk's office of the county where the land lies and for ten years thereafter, if not so dormant after the lapse of one year from date. Innkeepers have a special lien on all property deposited with them. Liverymen and proprietors of public stables have a special lien npon all animals and vehicles placed with them for amount of charges against same. Repairer of anything has a lien for the amount of his repairs. Employes of railroad have a prior lien on road and equipments for work done and tools and teams employed. Landlords have a prior lien on the property of the tenant for rents that are due or

WM. J. LEMP BREWING CO.'S

DALLAS BRANCH,

CHARLES MEISTERHANS, Agent.

A FULL SUPPLY OF

KEG AND BOTTLED Beer

CONSTANTLY ON HAND.

150 Ton Ice Factory in Connection.

DALLAS, ... TEXAS.

GRAND WINDSOR SHAVING PARLORS,

Artesian Baths, Hot and Cold.

First-Class Service. Polite Attention.

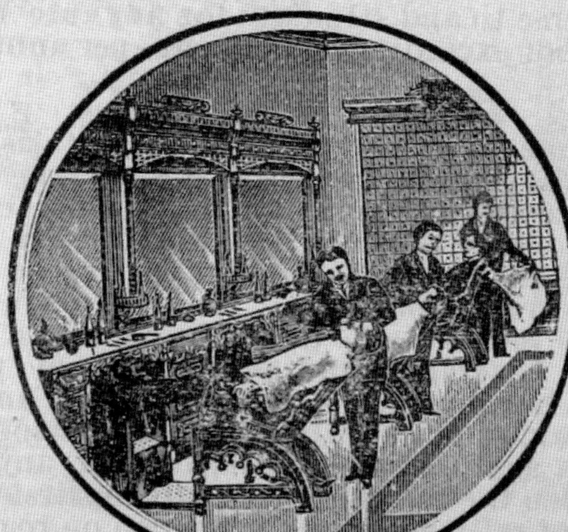

OPEN FROM 6:00 A. M. TO 9:00 P. M.

GEO. W. SHIRLEY, Proprietor.

GRAND WINDSOR HOTEL, Dallas, Texas.

may become due as long as the property remains on the rented premises and for one month thereafter. Owner of male animal has lien on progeny for his services for twelve months from the birth of such progeny.

Mechanics Contractors &c.: Anyone furnishing labor or material has a lien on the property for the same. The lien of an original contractor's must be filed within four months after indebtedness shall have accrued, all others thirty days, written notice must be given owner or his agent of material furnished. If on homestead, written contract signed and acknowledged by husband and wife and recorded is an esential prerequisite to fixing the lien.

All mortgage liens of personal property (chattel mortgages) to be valid against creditors and subsequent purchasers in good faith must be registered or followed by an actual continued change of possession. All mortgaged liens of real estate (deed of trust) must be recorded in the county clerk's office of the county where the land lies, in a book kept for that purpose. The vendor of real estate retains an implied lien on note for the payment thereof. Limitations to be relied on must be pleaded; does not run against married women, infants, insane persons and persons imprisoned. Cannot tack one disability to another.

LIMITATION OF ACTIONS ON LAND.

Every suit for the recovery of real estate as against any person in peaceable and adverse possession thereof under color or color of title shall be instituted within three years next after the cause of action shall have accrued.

Every suit for the recovery of real estate as against any person having peaceable and adverse possession thereof, cultivating, using or enjoying the same and paying taxes thereon, if any, and claiming under a deed or deeds duly registered shall be instituted within five years next after the cause of action shall have accrued. Any person who has the right of action for the recovery of any lands, tenements or

...Hughes Bros...

Manufacturing Co.

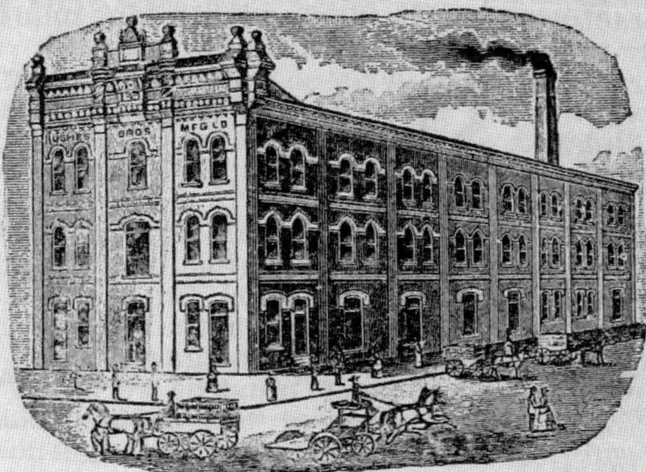

Manufacturers of

DR. HUGHES'

GRAPE ✦ BAKING ✦ POWDER

Every Can of which is Guaranteed.

Jelly, Preserves, Flavoring Extracts, Bluing, Cider, Apple and White Wine Vinegars and a full line of Grocers' Shelf Goods. All of our goods are guaranteed Pure, and are recognized as STANDARD QUALITY.

PATRONIZE YOUR HOME FACTORIES,

Writes Us for Prices Before Buying.

THE LARGEST FACTORY OF ITS KIND IN THE SOUTH.

or hereditaments against another having peaceable and adverse possession thereof, cultivating, using or enjoying the same, shall institute his suit therefor within ten years next after his cause of action shall have accrued.

PERSONAL ACTIONS.

There shall be presented within one year after the cause of action shall have accrued all actions or suits in court of the following description: Actions for injuries done to the person of another; for malicious prosecution or for injuries done to the character or reputation of another by libel or slander; for damages for seduction or breach of promise of marriage; for injuries done to the person of another where death results from such injuries, and the cause of action shall be considered as having accrued at the death of the party injured.

There shall be presented in two years after the cause of action shall have accrued all actions or suits in court of the following description: Actions of trespass, for injury done to the estate or the property of another; for detaining the personal property of another and for converting such personal property to one's own use; for taking or carrying away the goods and chattles of another: for debt when the indebtedness is not evidenced by a contract in writing upon stated or open account other than merchaedise accounts between merchants and merchant.

There shall be presented within four years after the cause of action shall have accrued, actions for debt when contract is in writing; for lands to convey real estate; on lands of executors, administrators and guardians; on merchandise accounts between merchant and merchant, and on partnership matters.

Every judgment rendered outside this state is governed by the limitation laws of the place where rendered.

Actions for the specific performance to convey real estate shall be brought in ten years.

L. J. BARTLETT,

ORIENTAL

Livery, Sale

and

Boarding Stable.

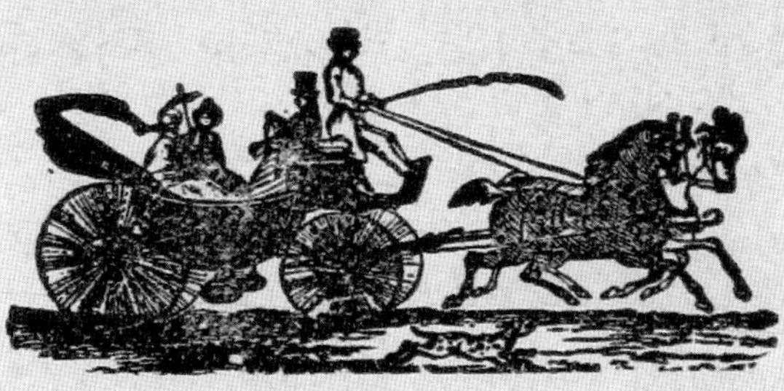

Everything NEW and First-Class.

Most Fashionable and Stylish Liveries in Texas.

CARRIAGES, BUGGIES, PHÆTONS,
SADDLE HORSES, Etc.
FURNISHED AT SHORT NOTICE

In connection with the Livery Business, we furnish Fine Carriages for Calling, Shopping, Balls and Theaters.

237, 239 and 241 Commerce St.,

Telephone 156. Dallas, Texas.

Dormant judgments may be revived by action of scire facias brought in ten years from date of judgment.

Actions against officers for failure to return execution must be brought within five years.

Actions for forceable entry or detainer must be brought in two years from the commission of the offense.

Actions to contest validity of will must be prosecuted within four years from its probate, and to cancel it for fraud must be brought in four years after its discovery.

SUFFRAGE.

Voter must have resided 12 months in state and six months in the county and be a resident of the election precinct in which he votes.

Registration a prerequisite to voting at any state, county or city election in cities having a population of 10,000 or over. Every male person not otherwise disqualified is entitled to register who shall have become of the age of 21 years by the day of election, A system of voting much like the Australian system prevails in Texas cities.

TAXES.

The rate of taxation in the City of Dallas, is $1.45 on the $100.00 worth of property. The combined state and county tax is 81 cents on the $100.00 worth of property.

USURY.

All written contracts whatsoever which may in any way directly or indirectly stipulate for a greater rate of interest than 10 per cent. per annum, shall be void and of no effect for the interest only, but the principal sum may be recovered.

A. H. PEACOCK,

Dealer in

...Watches...

Diamonds and Jewelry.

Repairing in all its Branches.

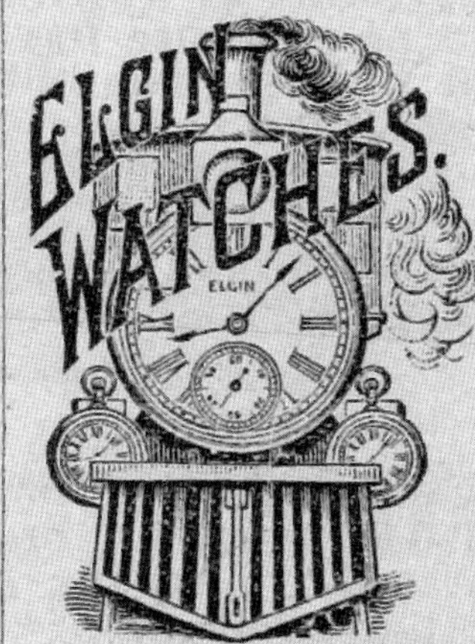

Work Guaranteed.

The Most Complete Line of

Gold, . Silver . and . Steel . Spectacles

IN THE STATE.

Spectacles Adjusted to any condition of the Eyes.

221 Elm Street, Near Lamar,

DALLAS, - TEXAS.

Ursuline Academy, DALLAS, TEXAS.

This institution, chartered by the legislature of the State, continues to afford that thorough and refined education which has distinguished it since its establishment in our city.

A Select Day School has been attached to the Academy. Studies will be resumed on Monday, Sept. 3.

TERMS, in advance, per session of 20 weeks, from Sept. to Feb., and from Feb. to the latter part of June:

Board, washing, tuition, elements of drawing, stationery, plain and fancy needle work and the ordinary infirmary expenses....$100 00
Entrance fee (only for the first year)..... ....$ 5 00
Graduating fee 5 00

EXTRA CHARGES.

Latin, per sessson of five months..... .... $15 00
Lessons on the Piano and use of instrument per session..................$30 00
Lessons on the Violin, per session...............$25 00

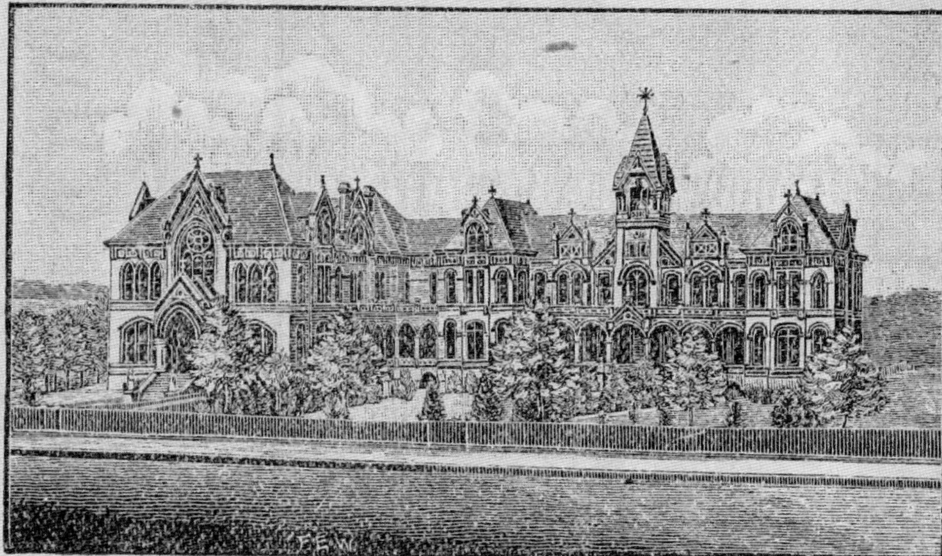

For particulars, apply to

MOTHER SUPERIOR, St. Joseph Street, between Live Oak and Bryan.

Business Directory

—OF THE—

ENTERPRISING BUSINESS

—AND—

Professional Men

—OF—

DALLAS, TEXAS.

The following Directory is for the benefit of those advertising in the Souvenir Guide of Dallas and shows where copies can be obtained and will be presented free with the compliments of the giver.

ADVERTISING AGENTS.

Robertson, Wyndham, (Street Car), 137 Main.

Robinson, Geo., Basement Trust Bldg.

AGRICULTURAL IMPLEMENTS.

Deering, Wm. & Co., 138-140 Camp St., corner Griffin; W. N. Stroud, Gen'l Agt.

Eagle Mfg. Co., R. W. Hanaway, Mgr.

Hatch, W. H., 136 Elm and 113 Jefferson.

Kanady Co., S. W., 523-527 Elm.

Keating Implement and Machine Co., 106-114 N. Jefferson.

Mansur & Tibbetts Implt. Co., 149-151 Elm; J. C. Duke, Mgr.

Parlin & Orendorff Co., 145-147 Elm; Wm. M. Robinson, Mgr.

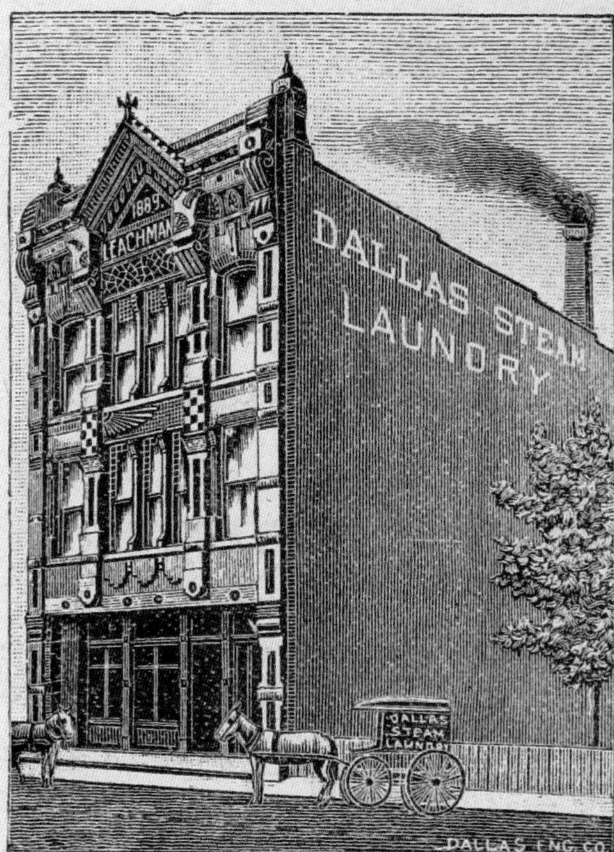

Dallas
Steam Laundry,

117 Live Oak Street. 400 Pacific Avenue.

G. S. LEACHMAN, Proprietor.

WANTS AN AGENT in every town where not now represented. It will pay a good man well. Largest Capacity and Best Work of any Laundry in the State.

Dyeing and Cleaning in Connection.

Southwestern Rock Island Plow Co., 125 Main, F. B. Jones, Sec.

Texas Implt. and Machine Co., Broadway, between Main and Elm.

Texas Moline Plow Co., cor. Main and Broadway.

ARCHITECTS AND SUPERINTENDENTS.

Silven, E. H. & Co., Cockrell Annex Bldg.

ARTESIAN WELL MACHINERY.

American Well Works, cor. Pacific Ave. and Lamar.

ARTIFICIAL LIMB MFRS.

Chapman, W. & E., 342 Elm.

AUCTIONEER.

HURD, J. M., 253 Elm.

BADGE AND BAGGAGE CHECKS.

Dallas Engraving and Mfg. Co., North Texas Bank Bldg.; F. L. Lake, Prop.

Edwards, Frank, North Texas Bank Bldg.

BAGGAGE TRANSFER.

Dallas Transfer and Cab Co., 144 S. Ervay.

BAKERIES.

Model Bakery, Chas. Goodman, Prop.; 377 Elm and 298 Main.

Queen City Bakery, P. H. Kleber & Son Proprietors; cor. Ervay and Marilla and 166 Griffin.

BAKING POWDER MFRS.

Hughes Bros. Mfg. Co., 417 S. Ervay, corner Hughes.

Can Fit You.

RUPTURE and PILES

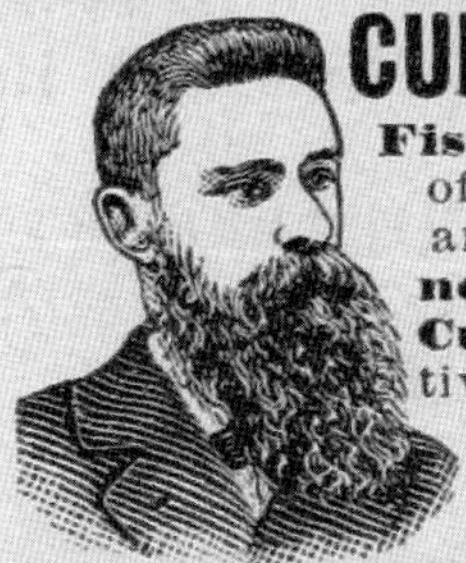

CURED Without the KNIFE or detention from business. **Fistula, Fissure, Ulceration** of the **Rectum, Hydrocele** and **Varicocele. No Cure no Pay**, and **No Pay until Cured**. Send stamp for descriptive pamphlet, containing certificates from many prominent people, some of whom you may know. Address,

DR. F. J. DICKEY, 395 Main St., Dallas, Tex.

THE BEST TRUSS MADE.

I. S. DICKERSON,

—DEALER IN—

Diamonds, Watches, Jewelry,

Guns, Pistols, Musical Instruments, etc.,

538 ELM STREET,

DALLAS, TEXAS.

T. B. BROWN,

DEALER IN

Staple and Fancy Groceries

Cor. Tenth and Lancaster, Oak Cliff, Texas.

DOCK & HENRY,

Shaving Parlor

Shaving, Shampooing and Hair Cutting,

LATEST STYLES.

Six First-Class Barbers and the Finest of Chairs.

Everything Neat and First-Class.

CALL AND SEE US. Satisfaction Guaranteed.

104 North Akard St., bet. Main and Elm Sts.

BANKS.

American National Bank, 225-227 Main, corner Poydras.

City National Bank, 277-279 Main, cor. Murphy.

Mercantile National Bank, 220 Elm; Joseph Huey, Pres.; A. V. Lane, Vice-Pres.; Paul Furst, Cashier.

National Bank of Commerce, 226 Elm, corner Poydras; J. B. Adoue, Pres.; J. D. Estes, cashier.

National Exchange Bank, 249-251 Main; John N. Simpson, Pres.; Royal A. Ferris, Cashr.

BARBERS.

Dock & Henry, 104 N. Akard.

Edward Gray, Prop. White Elephant, 307 Main.

Geo. W. Shirley, Prop. Grand Windsor Shaving Parlors, Main street.

T. E. Thomas, 496 Elm.

BOILER MAKERS AND REPAIRS.

Mosher Mfg. Co., 311-317 S. Lamar.

Central Boiler Works, W. H. Riley, Prop., 132 Austin.

BOILER PLATES AND FLUES.

Hetherington & Nason, 173-175 Elm.

Hunter & Booso, 172-174 Elm.

Mosher Mfg. Co., 311-317 S. Lamar.

BOOK BINDERS.

Hargreaves, Sam, 192 Main.

F. J. HENGY,
South Dallas Foundry
IRON AND BRASS CASTINGS.

All Kinds of Stove Repairs in Stock.

Central Avenue, Dallas, Texas.

(Cor. H. & T. C. and G. C. & S. F. R'y Crossing.)

F. J. HENGY,
WHOLESALE DEALER IN **SCRAP IRON**

METALS and OLD MACHINERY,

Bones and Empty Bottles,

335 to 340 Griffin Street, Dallas, Texas.

L. CRADDOCK,
...Wholesale...

Liquors
Wines and Cigars
227 Elm Street,

226 Pacific Avenue,

DALLAS, TEXAS.

BOOKSELLERS & STATIONERS.

Johnson, F. M., 106 N. Ervay.

Smith, J T. & Co., 266 Main.

BOOT AND SHOE FINDINGS.

Padgitt Bros., 248-250 Commerce.

Schœllkopf, G. H., 218-220 Commerce.

BEEF PACKERS.

Dallas Dressed Beef and Packing Co., 126-128 Alma., office 145 N. Akard; R. Myrick, Sec. and Mgr.

BILL POSTER.

Robinson, Geo., (City Bill Poster) office Mortgage & Trust Co's Bldg—basement.

BOOTS & SHOES—RETAIL.

Howell Bros., 288 Elm.

Kahn, Leon, 216 Elm.

Lowenstein, A., 506-508 Elm.

Newbury, Lee, cor. Elm and Murphy.

Robinson, B. T., 300 Elm.

Sanger Bros., 192-208 Elm, 199 201 Main and 109 N. Lamar.

Wasserman, M., Elm St., two blks. W. Union Depot.

BOOTS AND SHOES—WHOLESALE.

Howell Bros. Shoe Co., 288 Elm.

Sanger Bros., 180-182 Elm.

WEATHERINGTON · BROS.

PHOTOGRAPHERS & PHOTO-ENGRAVERS

321 ELM ST. DALLAS TEX.

BOTTLING WORKS.

Hughes Bros. Mfg. Co., corner S. Ervay and Hughes.

BOX MFRS.

Texas Paper Co., 95-97 Patterson Ave.

BREWERIES.

Lemp, W. J. Brewing Co., S. W. cor. T. & P. Ry. and Crowdus; Chas. Meisterhans, Mgr.

BUSINESS BUREAU.

Texas Business Bureau, J. W. Hudnall, Mgr., Room 517 North Texas Bank Bldg.

CANDY MAKER & CONFECTIONER.

Garlington, M. D., & Co., 130-132 Camp, cor. Patterson Ave.

CARPETS.

Sanger Bros., 192-208 Elm.

Texas Installment Co., J. F. Zang, Proprietor, 251-253 Elm and 2.0-252 Pacific Ave.

CARRIAGE PAINTERS.

Lander, M. R. & Co., 103 Camp.

Meserole Bros., 405 Elm.

Reynolds & Johnson, 111 Camp.

CARRIAGES & VEHICLES.

Eagle Mfg. Co., R. W. Hanaway, Mgr.

Hatch, W. H., 113-115 Jefferson and 136-142 Elm.

Kanady Co. S. W., 523-527 Elm.

Special Reasons

For Insuring

IN THE

Union Central

I It is organized under **Ohio Laws**. Hence,

1 It cannot make risky investments. Its securities are mostly mortgages on real estate **worth in cash double the amount loaned thereon**, exclusive of buildings.

2. **Stockholders are responsible** to the Policy-holders for twice their stock.

3. An **Annual Examination** of the Company's affairs is made by the State Commissioner.

4. It must hold for protection of Policy-holders a **Reserve at Four per cent.**—the highest rate.

II It is a **Western Company**. Hence,

1. It has great advantages in loaning money.

2. It can invest its money where it obtains it. In this it is unlike Eastern Companies.

3. It secures the highest rate of interest of any Company in the United States.

III It is **liberal in its methods**.

1. It avoids legal contests.

2 It continues its Policies in case of lapse until the value of the Reserve is exhausted.

3. It pays losses promptly, and before due.

IV It is **Well Managed.** Hence,

1 Its death rate for many years has been the lowest in the land.

2. It has had the most rapid increase of business.

3 It pays large dividends on dividend policies.

4. It offers the **Guaranty Policy**, the best known for Life and Term Insurance, at low rates, and the **Life-Rate Endowment**, the best for Endowment at small cost. For terms of contract, call on or address

JESSE F. MYERS, General Agent,

SHERMAN, TEXAS.

CARRIAGES & VEHICLES.—CONTINUED.

Keating Implmt. & Machine Co., 106-114 N. Jefferson, cor. Elm.

Mansur & Tebbetts Implt. Co., 149-151 Elm; J. C. Duke, Mgr.

Padgitt Bros., 248-250 Commerce.

Parlin & Orendorff Co., 145-147 Elm: Wm. M. Robinson, Mgr.

Southern Rock Island Plow Co., 125 Main.

Texas Implement & Machine Co., Broadway bet. Main and Elm.

Texas Moline Plow Co., cor. Main and Broadway.

Witwer, John S., 275 Elm and 276 Pacific Ave.

CHINA, GLASS & QUEENSWARE.

Doolittle, Simpson & Co., 311-316 Elm (Arcade).

Walker's China Hall, 248 Elm; J. B. Cummins, Proprietor.

CIDER & EXTRACT MFRS.

Hughes Bros. Mfg. Co., cor. Ervay & Hughes.

Star Mfg. Co., 335 Main.

CIGARS & TOBACCOS.

Bejano & Delgado, 318 Main.

Bell, Wm. R., 113 Houston.

Brown, T. B., Oak Cliff.

Eason. H. H., 111 S. Ervay.

Live Oak Grocery, T. F. Loughlin, Propr., 381 383 Elm.

Parks & Bradford, cor. Elm and Akard.

The Star Mfg. Co., 335 Main.

Williams & Williams, 231 Elm.

CLOTHING.

Kahn, E. M. & Co., 212-214 Elm, cor. N. Lamar.

Lowenstein, A., 506-508 Elm.

Robinson, B. T., 304 Elm.

Sanger Bros., 192-208 Elm, 199-201 Main, 109 N. Lamar.

Salzenstein, C., 236 Elm (The Model).

Wasserman, M., Elm St., two blks. W. Union Depot.

WHOLESALE.

Sanger Bros., 192-208 Elm, 199-201 Main, 109 N. Lamar.

COAL DEALERS.

Reid, W., North Texas Bank Bldg.

Standard Coal Yard, cor. Jackson & Lamar, cor. Pacific Ave. and Cantegral.

COAL OIL DEALERS.

Eagle Refining Co., A. W. Clem, Mgr.

Hurst, John M , 409 Main (Coal Oil John.)

CONTRACTORS.

Ashton, C., Oak Cliff.

Barker & Kline, 472 Main.

Beilharz, T. M., (stone) cor. Pacific Ave. and N. Hawkins.

Hartman, C. S., cor. Armstrong & Kentucky.

Hurley, R. J., 221 Texas.

Ragland, T. F., 362 Commerce.

Slaughter & Mottwiler, 362 Commerce.

Stubbs, G. W. & Sons, 263 Holmes.

Watson, A., 135 Sanger Ave.

Whitlock & Sunderland, 472 Main.

COMMISSION MERCHANTS.

Garlington, M. D., 203-205 Commerce.

Jackson, A. A. & Co., 345-347 Elm.

COLLEGES & SCHOOLS.

Dallas Telegraph College, L. C. Robinson, Prop., 569 Elm.

Cole's Private School, San Jacinto.

The Lone Star School of Oratory, Music and Bible Lectures, cor. Elm and Harwood.

Ursuline Academy, St. Joseph street, bet. Live Oak & Bryan.

COTTON AND WOOLEN GOODS MFRS.

Dallas Cotton Mills, on Corinth, bet. Cockrell and S. Austin; W. C. Howard, Pres.

DENTISTS.

Blair, R. H., Room 301 North Tex. Bank Bldg.

Storey, J. C., over 213 Main.

Tichenor, J. L. 569 Elm.

Wilkins, Geo., 291 Elm.

Holsey, Dr. J. H., 497 Main.

DEPOSIT VAULTS.

Security, Mortgage & Trust, corner Main and Austin.

DIRECTORY PUBLISHERS.

The D. M. Anderson Directory Co., 282 Main.

DOOR AND WINDOW SCREEN MFRS.

Dallas Screen Works, G. E. Rust, prop., cor. Ross Ave. and N. Akard.

DRESS MAKERS.

Findley, Mrs., 444 Main.

Sanger Bros., 192-208 Elm.

Stewart, Mrs. E. C., 395 Main.

DRUGGISTS.

Bumpas & Kirby, 177 Main.

Elite Pharmrcy, 145 S. Ervay.

Palace Drug Store, Shook & Cooper, Proprs., 271 Main.

Trinity Drug Store, 384 Elm.

DRY GOODS AND NOTIONS—RETAIL.

Goldsmith, I. & Co., 244-246 Elm.

Harris, A. & Co., 266, 268 and 270 Elm.

Lowenstein, A., 506-508 Elm.

Robinson, B. P., 304 Elm

Sanger Bros., 192-208 Elm.

Wasserman, M., 502 Elm.

WHOLESALE.

Sanger Bros. 192-208 Elm.

DYEING AND REPAIRING.

Ellis, J. D., 307 Elm.

Hill, J. T. W., 368 Main.

ELECTRIC SUPPLIES.

Hunter & Booso, 172-174 Elm.

ENGINES, BOILERS AND MACHINERY.

American Well Works Co., 191 Elm, corner Austin, H. H. Jones, Mgr.

Hetherington & Nason, 173-175 Elm.

Hunter & Booso, 172-174 Elm.

Keating Implement & Machine Co., 106-114 N. Jefferson, cor. Elm.

Mosher Mfg. Co., 311-317 S. Lamar.

ENGRAVERS.

Wetherington Bros, 321 Elm.
Giraud, Paul, 313 Main.

FEED, HAY & GRAIN.

Holloway & Co., 644 Elm.
Pittman & Harrison. cor. Elm and Ervay.

FISH AND OYSTERS.

Hunt Bros., S. Ervay bet. Commerce & Jackson
Hunt, Wm., 580 Elm.
Nussbaumer & Co., 152 Main.
Post-Office Meat Market, 105 S. Ervay.
Standard Market, 107 S. Ervay; C. H. Williams, Prop.

FLORISTS.

Johnson's Flower Store, 340 Main.

FRUITS AND CONFECTIONERIES.

Bejano & Delgado, 318 Main.
Eason, H. H., 111 Ervay.
Hunt, Wm., 580 Elm.

FUNERAL DIRECTORS.

Linskie, P. W., 465 Main.
Smith, Ed C. & Bro., S. Ervay.

FURNISHED ROOMS.

Findley, Mrs. M. P., 444 Main.
Marks, Mrs. Annie; 431 Commerce.

FURNITURE DEALERS.

Texas Installment Co., J. F. Zang; 251-253 Elm

FURNITURE MOVERS.

Dallas Moving & Storage Co., 369 Elm; W. H. Darrah, Mgr.

GENT'S FURNISHING GOODS.

Kahn, E. M. & Co., 212-214 Elm.

Mittenthall, H. S. & Co., 229 Elm.

Robinson, B. T., 304 Elm

Sanger Bros., 192-208 Elm, 199-201 Main.

Salzenstein, Chas. Prop., 233 Elm (The Model)

GRAIN DEALERS.

Pittman & Harrison, cor. Elm & Ervay.

GRINDERS AND SAW FILERS.

Corrie, John H., 111 N. Akard.

GROCERS.

Best, W. E. & Sons, 161 Ross Ave.

Bell, Wm. R., 113 South Houston.

Brown, T. B., Oak Cliff.

Holloway & Co., 644 Elm.

Live Oak Grocery, T. F. Loughlin Proprietors, 381-383 Elm.

Parks & Bradford, cor. Elm and Akard.

Williams & Williams, 201 Elm.

Wunderlich, Emil, 158 Main.

WHOLESALE.

Parks & Bradford, cor. Elm and Akard.

Loughlin, Thos. F., 381-383 Elm.

HAIR DRESSERS & DEALERS.

Clever, Miss M. L., 318 Elm.

HARDWARE & CUTLRY.

(WHOLESALE AND RETAIL.)

Robinson, Bird & Co., 308-310 Elm.

HARNESS & SADDLES.

Kanady Co., S. W., 523-527 Elm.
Meserole Bros., 405 Elm.
Padgitt Bros, 248-250 Commerce.
Witte & Darwin, 479 Elm.

HAT MFRS.

Wood & Edwards, 344 Main.

HORSE COLLAR MFRS.

Schœllkopf, G. H., 218 220 Commerce.
Padgitt Bros., 248-250 Commerce.

HORSESHOERS.

Eeles, Harry, 522 Elm
Mansfield, S. G., 125 Poydras
Munckton Bros., 221 North Akard
Reynolds & Johnson, 111 Camp

HOUSE FURNISHING GOODS.

The Great Southern Furnishing Co., H. B. Criswell, Mgr.; 371 Elm.
Texas Installment Co., 251-253 Elm; J. F. Zang

OYSTER & ICE CREAM PARLORS.

Bejano & Delgado, 318 Main
Parrott, Mrs. Ida L., (The Pearl) Akard, bet. Main and Commerce.

ICE MFRS. AND DEALERS.

Dallas Ice Factory & Cold Storage Co.

Lemp, W. J. Brewing Co., (New Ice Co.) East Dallas.

INK ROLLER FACTORY.

Bradfield's Texas Roller Factory, 337 Pacific Ave.

INSURANCE AGENTS

Leonard, H M. Gen'l Agent Home Life Insurance Co, 341 Main

Myers, Jesse F., (Sherman) Gen'l Agent Central Union

Thomas Bros., (Fire Insurance) 312 Main

INVESTMENT COMPANIES

American Investment Co, Rooms 203-206 Exchange Bank Bld'g; Elliott & Price, Mgrs

JEWELERS—Wholesale

Linz, Joseph & Bro, 312 Main

JEWELERS & WATCHMAKERS

Beck, S, 215 Main
Dickerson, I. S., 538 Main
Peacock, A. H., 221 Elm

JOBBERS & FURNISHING GOODS

Rose, B W & Co, 191-193 Elm

JUNK DEALERS

Hengy, F J, 335-337 Griffin

LADIES' WEAR & FURNISHING GOODS

Goldsmith, I. & Co, 244-246 Elm
Harris, A. & Co, 266 270 Elm
Sanger Bros., 190 208 Elm

LAUNDRIES

Dallas Steam Laundry, G. S. Leachman, Prop 117 Live Oak

LAWYERS

Ball, A. J., 293 Main
Bell & Atwell, 220 Main
Coombes & Coombes, 179 Main.
Davis & Astin, 175 Main
Davis, J. O., 220 Main
Edwards, W. M., 179 Main
Evans, Chas. I., Room 520 North Texas Bank Bld'g
Gill & Clanton, 177 Main
Merchant, W. B., 281 Main
Miller & Williams, cor. Main and Houston
Robertson, M. L., 249 Main
Rœhrig, Chas. F., 233 Main
Smith, Curtis, P., 257 Main
Wiley, J. E., 323 Elm

LEATHER & SHOE FINDINGS

Padgitt Bros., 248-250 Commerce
Schœllkopf, G. H., 218-220 Commerce

FRED'S PLACE,

GENT'S RESTAURANT.
LADIES' DINING PARLOR.

Attentive Waiters, Electric Fans.
Cool and Neat.

Short Orders and Meals at all Hours, at Low Rates. Try us once and you will come again.

Mr. and Mrs. SMALLEY, Proprs.,

382 Main St., DALLAS, TEXAS.

USE P. AMATO'S

ITALIAN HAIR RESTORER

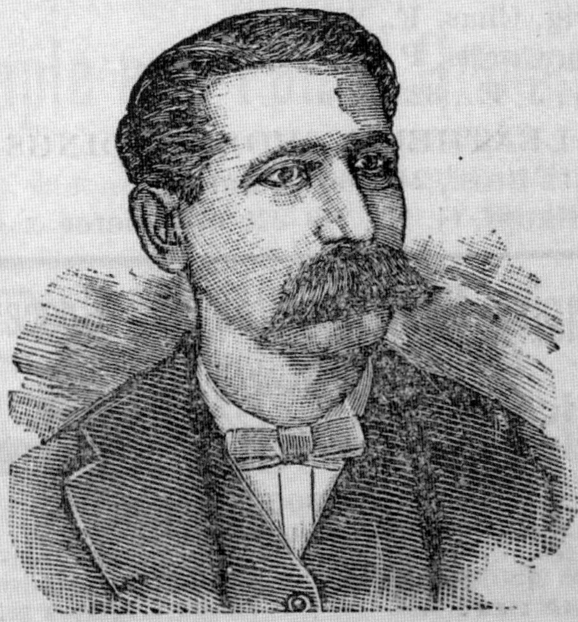

P. AMATO, Sole Proprietor,
216 South Akard St., DALLAS, TEXAS.
For sale by all Druggists.

LIQUORS, WINES AND CIGARS.

(WHOLESALE.)

Bruce, M. T. & Co., 217 Elm and 216 Pacific Ave.

Craddock, C., 227 Elm, 226 Pacific Ave

T. F. Loughlin, (Live Oak Grocery) 381-383 Elm

LIVE STOCK BREEDERS AND DEALERS.

Lomo Alto Stock Farm. Henry Exall, Mgr.; office 310 North Texas Bank Bld'g

Hill, W. M. C. (Postmaster.)

LIVERY, SALE AND FEED STABLES.

Bartlett, L. J., 237-241 Commerce

LUMBER AND SHINGLES.

Jones, M. T. Lumber Co, cor Main, Elm and St. Paul Sts

MACHINISTS.

Dillon Machine Co., 107 Market

Mosher Mfg. Co., 311-317 South Lamar

MEAT MARKETS.

Nussbaumer, & Co., 152 Main

Post-Office Meat Market, 105 South Ervay; W. J. McCray, Prop

Standard Market, 107 South Ervay; C. H. Williams, Prop.

Empire Meat Market and Grocery, 158 Main; Emil Wunderlich, Prop.

MECHANICAL ENGINEERS.

Hunter & Booso, 172-174 Elm

MEDICAL INSTITUTES FOR LIQUOR & MORPHINE HAPITS.

The Dallas Ensor Institute, 287 Elm; C. B. Beard, Mgr

The Hagey Institute, Main street

MERCHANT TAILORS.

Herman Tailoring Co., 258 Elm.

Stuart, C. H. 114 South Akard

MESSENGER SERVICE.

Dallas Messenger Service, North Texas Bank

MILLINERY & FANCY GOODS.

Ferrell, Madame, 318 Elm

Goldsmith, I. & Co., 244-248 Elm

Sanger Bros., 192-208 Elm

MODEL MAKERS.

Texas Pattern & Model Works, 339 Pacific Ave A. Giacomini, Prop.

MUSICAL INSTRUMENTS.

Chicago Cottage Organ Co., 341 Main

Dickerson, I. S., 538 Elm

Edwards, C. H., 262-267 Main

Goggan, Thos. & Bro., 231 Elm

Hollingsworth, Bullington & Co., 261 Main

MUSIC PUBLISHERS.

The Showalter-Lincoln Publishing Co., 216 Main

MUSIC TEACHERS.

Benham & Turner, Scollard Bld'g, Room 209

NEWSPAPERS.

Dallas Morning News—established 1885—Daily issued every morning; weekly Thursday, office. 199-201 Commerce. A. H. Belo & Co., Pub'rs.; Geo. B. Dealey, Bus. Mgr.

Dallas Times-Herald, issued every evening except Sunday, weekly Saturday. office, S. Ervay Published by the the Times-Herald Pub. Co.

Southern Mercury—issued every Thursday, 192 main—Milton Parks, managing editor and business manager

NEWSPAPERS (Continued).

Texas Baptist and Herald, issued every Thursday—office 358 Main. S. A. and A. R. Hayden, Proprs. and Publishers

Texas Farm and Ranch, issued every Saturday, office 343 Main. Texas Farm and Ranch Pub. Co.

Texas Farmer, issued every Saturday; office, 369 371 Elm. Texas Farmer Co., Proprs. and Mgr's; Shaw & Blaylock, publishers

Texas Health Journal, Briggs, Pipkin, Rucker & Elmore, Propr's; office 315, 317 and 318 North Texas Bank Bld'g. Issued Monthly

The Advance, issued weekly, 192 Main

Texas Sandwich, issued weekly by the Texas Sandwich Publishing Co.; presiding elder, S. A. Fishburn

OIL DEALERS.

Eagle Refining Co., O. P. I. Buell, Mg'r, 212 Security, Mortgage & Trust Bld'g

Hurst, John M.,—Coal Oil John—409 Main

Waters-Pierce Oil Co., cor Cochran and Jefferson; Wm. Grice, Mgr.

OMNIBUS AND BAGGAGE

Dallas Transfer Co., 144 S Ervay

PAINT MFRS.

Western Paint Co., 403 Elm: F. T. Des Brisay, Mg'r

PAINTS, OILS & PAINTERS SUPPLIES.

Black, A. P. 383 Elm

Western Paint Co., 403 Elm

PAINTERS & PAPER HANGERS

Barker, L. W., Barker & Kline

Ragland, T. F., 352 Commerce

PAPER, PAPER BOXES AND TWINE.

Dorsey, J. A. & Co., 247-249 Elm

Texas Paper Co., 95 97 Patterson Ave., corner Griffin

PHONOGRAPHERS

Baldwin & Co. B. A., 104½ N Ervay

PHRENOLOGISTS

Henry, Prof. A., 448 Main

PHOTOGRAPHERS

Bedford, T. J., 504 Elm
Chalmers, 304 Elm
Church, Clifton, 278 Elm
Weatherington Bros, 321 Elm

PHOTOGRAPHIC MATERIAL

Blessing, S T., 461 Elm

PHYSICIANS AND SURGEONS

Ashton, Lawrence, 455 Commerce
Dickey, F. J., 395 Main
Edmonson, M. M., office 3rd flo'r Trust Co. Bldg
Elmore, A. M., rooms 316, 317 and 318 North Texas Bank Bld'g
Lane, W. J., 213 Main
Steakley, Wm. W., 296 Main

PIANOS AND ORGANS.

Chicago, Cottage Organ Co., 341 Main
Edwards, C. H., 265-267 Main
Goggan, Thos. & Bro., 231 Elm
Hollingsworth, Bulington & Co., 216 Main

PICTURE COPYING & ENLARGING.

Anderson, C. B., & Co., 400 Elm
Weatherington Bros., 321 Elm

RAILROAD TICKET AGENTS.

Abel. W. H. Southwestern Pass. & Tkt. Agt., Chicago & Alton Ry., Windsor Hotel

Archer. H. C, Southwestern Pass & Tkt Agt., Baltimore & Ohio Ry., Windsor Hotel

Meslier, Gaston, Gen Pass & Tkt. Agent, Texas & Pacific Ry., Gould Bld'g

Turner, E. P., City Ticket Agt. T. & P. Ry.. 195 Main

Wilkins, Walter G.. City Ticket Agent Gulf, Colo. & Santa Fe Ry., Windsor Hotel

Kaiser, A., (Ticket Broker) 236 Main.

REAL ESTATE & RENTAL AGENTS.

Alexander, C. H., Field street

Gillespie & Cullum, 101 Austin

Metropolitan Land Bureau, L. A. Wilson, Mg'r 281 Main

McEnnis, Thos. F. 313 Main

Powell, E. M., 401 Main

Seay & Terry, 223 Main

Robertson & Weil, 105 Poydras

Thomas Bros., 312 Main

Thomas, J. F. 484 Main

Weatherington, A. J., 321 Elm

Wiley, J E., 322 Elm

RESTAURANTS

The Sun, 484 Elm: Lee Patrick, Propr

Fred's Place, 382 Main

ROAD MACHINE MFRS.

American Road Machine Co., 181 Elm; F. T. Woodward, Mg'r

RUBBER STAMP MFRS.

Dallas Engraving & Mfg. Co., North Texas Bank Bldg.

SCREEN MFRS.

Dallas Screen Co., cor. Ross Ave. & N. Akard

SEED DEALERS.

Holloway & Co., 292 Elm

SHIRT MFRS.

Vendig Bros, 224 Elm

STENOGRAPHERS

Evans & Morris, room 219 Trust Co. Bld'g

Lindsey, G. M. General Delivery

STONE SAW MILLS

Beilharz T. M., nw. cor. Pacific Ave.

STOVE REPAIRERS

DeMay, E. A., 135 N. Akard

STOVES AND TINWARE

Robinson, Bird & Co., 328-310 Elm

Shannon, Frank, 269 Elm

TINWARE MFRS.

Dallas Tinware Mfg. Co., 107 Patterson Ave

TRANSFER LINES

Red Line Transfer Co., 105 S. Lamar.

Dallas Transfer, Co., 144 S. Ervay

Dallas Transfer and Storage Co., 181 Elm

TYPEWRITERS.

Remington Standard, 243 Main; Merchant & Manning.

UNDERTAKERS

Linskie, P. W., 465 Main

Smith, Ed C. & Bro., S. Ervay.

WATCHES. CLOCKS & JEWELRY.

Beck, S, 215 Main

Crower & Bro., 116 S. Akard

Dickerson, I. S., 538 Main

Hurd, J. M., 253 Elm

Peacock, A. H., 221 Elm

YEAST MFRS.

Fleischman & Co., 145½ N. Akard; H. H. Frey,

ADDITIONAL.

DRUGGISTS.

Owl Pharmacy, cor. Ross Ave. and Griffin

Rogers, Russell V., Elm and Akard

The Oriental Drug Store, cor. Com'rce & Akard

HOTELS.

Merchants' Hotel, 194-196 Pacific Ave.

Queen City Hotel, 487 Elm

HAIR RESTORER MFR

Amato P., 216 S. Akard

GRAVEL AND COMPOSITION ROOFERS.

Dougherty & Buckelew, 371 Main

Plows Fine Candies.

PLOWS FINE CANDIES.

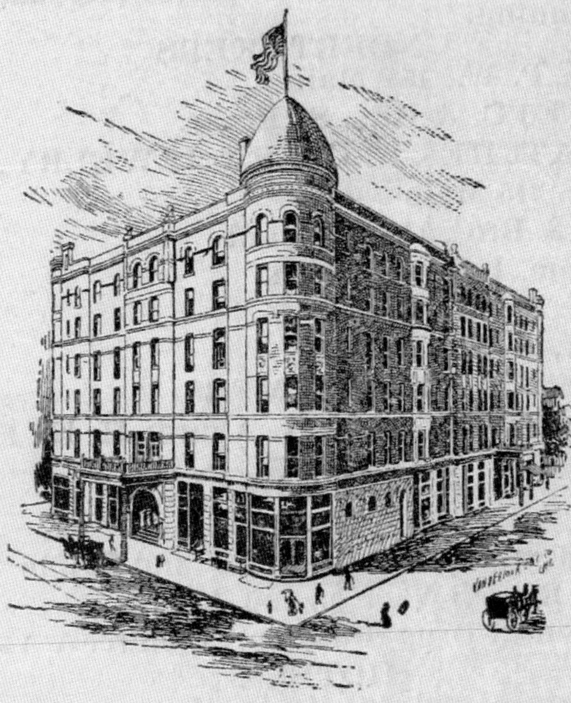

PLOWS FINE CANDIES.

The Oriental Drug Store,

ROBERT C. KOPISCH, Prop.

Cor. Commerce and Akard Sts , Oriental Hotel Bldg.

Pure . Drugs, . Toilet . Articles,
Fine . Chemicals,

Soda, Mineral Waters and Cigars.

Your Prescriptions Respectfully Solicited.

Telephone 521. Dallas, Texas.

INDEX TO ADVETISEMENTS.

Chicago Cottage Organ Co.

OF CHICAGO,

Are Represented in Dallas, Texas, At 341 Main Street.

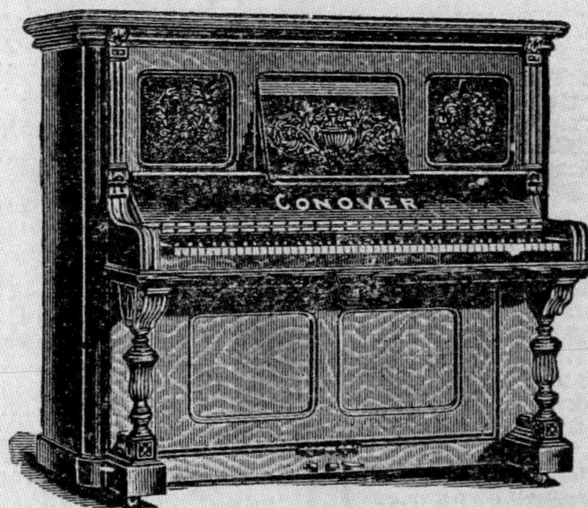

If you want a High-Grade PIANO,
If you want a Medium-Grade PIANO,
If you want a First-Class ORGAN,

If you want Goods that will prove as represented in every respect, you will find just what you want with us, and besides you will buy DIRECT from factory.

Yours respectfully,

Chicago Cottage Organ Co.

341 Main Street, DALLAS, TEXAS.

☞ See Robertson & Weil's "ad." on page 184.

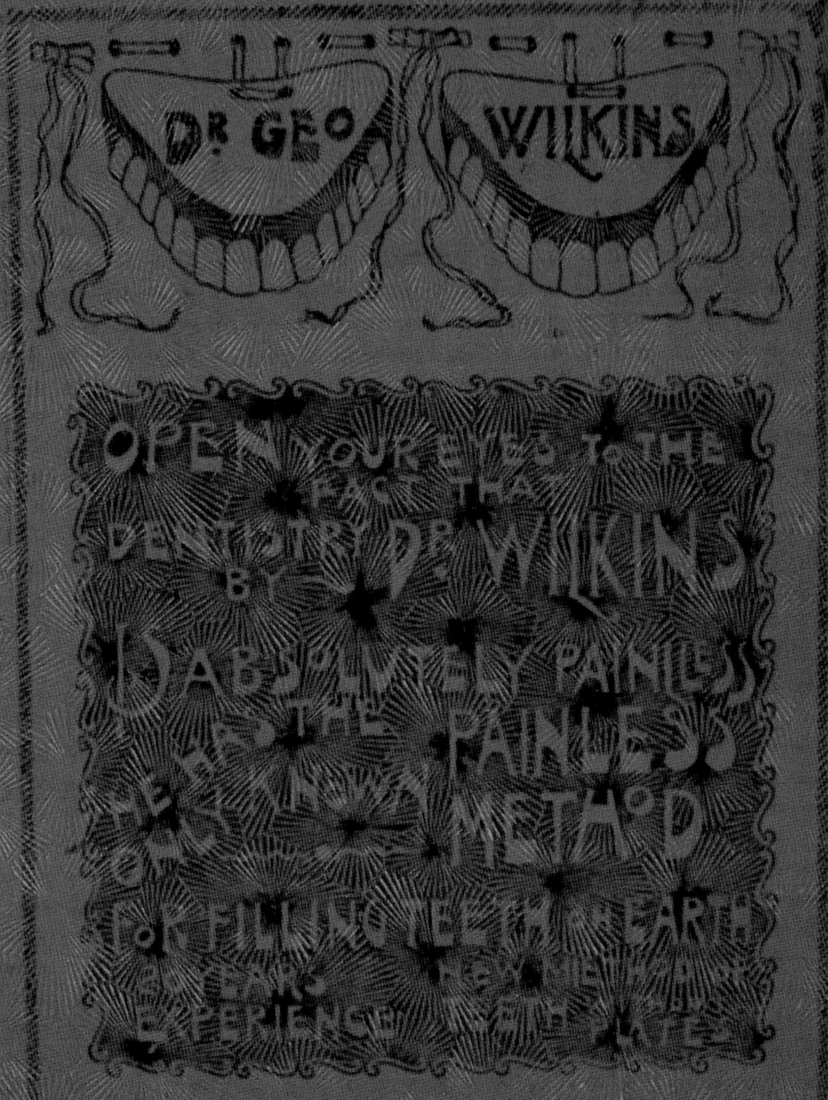

DR GEO
WILKINS
OPEN YOUR EYES TO THE
FACT THAT
DENTISTRY
BY
DR WILKINS
ABSOLUTELY PAINLESS
THE
PAINLESS
METHOD
FOR FILLING TEETH
EARTH
YEARS
EXPERIENCE
RATES
ST
DALLAS
TEX.